Joseph A. Hegarty, EdD

Standing the Heat
Assuring Curriculum Quality in Culinary Arts and Gastronomy

Pre-publication
REVIEWS,
COMMENTARIES,
EVALUATIONS . . .

"The age-old 'head versus hand' debate surrounding maturing professional education programs has finally been brought into a realistic perspective by Joseph Hegarty in *Standing the Heat.* Culinarians of the millennium are increasingly being asked to integrate their craft with the scientific developments through what Benjamin Bloom identified as 'higher order thinking skills.'

Several chapters can be used as a template for other programs attempting to expand and enlarge their vocational education programs. This text provides the genesis of a well-researched, thoughtful, rigorous, and sound theoretical framework for the enlargement and expansion of culinary arts and gastronomy higher education programs."

John M. Antun, PhD
Founding Director, National Restaurant Institute, School of Hotel, Restaurant, and Tourism Management,
University of South Carolina

"Finally, the heart of the house is getting the same attention the front the house has been getting for years. Chefs are managers and leaders. In many operations they are accountable for more labor dollars and expense dollars than any other single manager. Why we have relegated them to a pseudo-vocational education through the years is beyond me.

Joseph Hegarty has given us a road map to follow that will allow many institutions to upgrade the quality of education in culinary programs and allow chefs to sit at the leadership table as academic equals. Recognizing and holding chefs accountable for their management decisions and actions will only enhance the position and attract more individuals to the field of culinary arts and science. We applaud Dr. Hegarty for his efforts and his gift to the profession."

Duncan R. Dickson
Assistant Professor,
Rosen School of Hospitality Management,
University of Central Florida

"This very interesting and useful study of curriculum development, by Joseph Hegarty, is a detailed analysis of culinary arts education and how it can become established in higher education. It tells a fascinating story of how a curriculum for a new undergraduate degree in culinary arts was designed, developed, and introduced into a higher education institute of technology. It builds on this experience to propose the further development of culinary arts and gastronomy as a discipline in graduate professional programs at the masters and doctoral levels. The book is strong empirically in its use of observation and documentary sources and case study approaches. It also engages compellingly with a range of key theoretical issues relating to liberal and vocational education, professionalism, assessment, and curriculum development to demonstrate the broader significance of this experience. The chapters recounting the introduction of the undergraduate degree are especially intriguing, and the discussion of new directions for further study provides a challenging note on which to conclude the work.

The achievement of the work is twofold. It shows that in developing new curricula and structures it is necessary to be able to 'stand the heat,' and offers useful clues on how to do so. At the same time, for the pioneers of culinary arts education, it suggests ways of getting out of the kitchen and into advanced study that will respect the skills, creativity, and craft of a changing profession. This is a major achievement and deserves careful attention from all who are involved in similar enterprises."

Gary McCulloch
Professor of Education
University of Sheffield

"*Standing the Heat* is a valuable resource for anyone designing a curriculum. Although it is based on building quality into culinary arts and gastronomy education, the framework presented is useful for any field of study. This book effectively addresses the questions that need to be asked when designing a curriculum, evaluates a variety of assessment models, discusses the required validation checks and internal and external monitoring of the curriculum, and examines the introduction of graduate programs into culinary arts.

Hegarty addresses many issues that generally are not discussed in culinary education. The book provides an example curriculum that was designed for a specific institution, and in so doing, explores the tensions and constraints that guide (and many times hinder) the advancement of culinary arts education. The most valuable accomplishment of this book is that it forces the reader to think outside the conventional culinary arts framework and consider exciting opportunities for study and research in this emerging discipline."

Robert J. Harrington, PhD, CEC
Dean and Professor of the Chef
John Folse Culinary Institute
at Nicholls State University,
Thibodaux, Louisiana

The Haworth Hospitality Press®
An Imprint of The Haworth Press, Inc.
New York • London • Oxford

Standing the Heat
Assuring Curriculum Quality in Culinary Arts and Gastronomy

Standing the Heat
Assuring Curriculum Quality in Culinary Arts and Gastronomy

Joseph A. Hegarty, EdD

THHP

The Haworth Hospitality Press®
An Imprint of The Haworth Press, Inc.
New York • London • Oxford

Published by

The Haworth Hospitality Press®, an imprint of The Haworth Press, Inc., 10 Alice Street, Binghamton, NY 13904-1580.

Text in Chapter 5 has been quoted from *Millennium: Journal of International Studies.* This article first appeared in *Millennium,* Volume 20, Number 3, 1991, and is reproduced with the permission of the publisher.

Cover design by Lora Wiggins.

Library of Congress Cataloging-in-Publication Data

Hegarty, Joseph.
    Standing the heat: Assuring curriculum quality in culinary arts and gastronomy / Joseph A. Hegarty.
        p. cm.
Includes bibliographical references and index.
    ISBN 0-7890-1897-7 (hard : alk. paper)—ISBN 0-7890-1898-5 (soft : alk. paper)
    1. Hospitality industry—Study and teaching (Higher) I. Title.
    TX911.5.H44 2003
    647.94'071'1—dc21
                                          2003001807

To Eileen

ABOUT THE AUTHOR

Joseph Hegarty, MEd, EdD, has headed the School of Culinary Arts and Food Technology at the Dublin Institute of Technology Faculty of Food and Tourism since 1972. A Fellow of the Irish Hotel and Catering Institute, he is past president of the European Federation of the International Council on Hotel, Restaurant & Institutional Education (EuroCHRIE), Director-at-Large of CHRIE International, and Vice-President of Association Mondiale pour la Formation Hôtelière et Touristique (AMFORHT).

Dr. Hegarty is co-author of *The Story of the Dublin Institute of Technology and Academic Quality Assurance in Irish Higher Education: Elements of a Handbook.* He was joint winner of the Dean Robert A. Beck Journalism Award in 1995 and received the EuroCHRIE 2000 Achievement Award for Excellence in Food and Beverage Teaching. Dr. Hegarty is co-editor of the *Journal of Culinary Science* (Haworth).

CONTENTS

Acknowledgments   ix

Introduction   1

**Chapter 1. Culinary Arts As a Profession:
Possibilities and Prospects**   5

The Liberal/Vocational Debate in Culinary Arts   5
Relative Importance of Liberal and Vocational Education
   in Culinary Arts   8
Professional, Professionalism, and Professionalization
   in Culinary Arts   12
Four Essential Criteria for Distinguishing Professional
   Occupations   16

**Chapter 2. Culinary Arts Curriculum Development:
The Heart of the Educational Enterprise**   19

Toward a Definition of Curriculum   19
Curriculum Development—The Process   20
Recognizing the Master Performer   30
Curriculum Design for Deep Learning   30
Assessment and Examination of Different Kinds
   of Learning   32

**Chapter 3. Framework for the Development and Validation
of a New Culinary Arts Degree Program**   37

Culinary Arts Program Conception   37
The Preliminary Program Proposal   39
Preparation of the Program Documentation   41
Validation and Accreditation   43
Summary   51

**Chapter 4. Guidelines for Quality Assurance in Curriculum
Development for Culinary Arts Degree**   53

Quality Assurance in Curriculum Implementation
   and Management   53
Assessments and Examinations   57
Disciplinary Procedures   67
Student Appeals   69

Annual Monitoring Report   70
Consideration of the Annual Monitoring Report   74
Program Review   78
Termination of a Program   79

**Chapter 5. The Role of Reflexivity in Assuring Curriculum
Quality in Culinary Arts**   **81**

Reflection, Reflexivity, Reflective Thinking:
   A Never-Ending Dance   82
Advantage of Reflective Ethnography in Culinary
   Arts Curriculum Development   83
Problem Solving or Critical Theory in Culinary Arts
   Education   86

Chapter 6. The Curriculum Journey   **89**

Introduction   89
The Chronology of the Curriculum Development Process
   (May 1996 to May 1998)   89
Conclusion   120

**Chapter 7. Assuring Curriculum Quality in Graduate
Diplomas and Master's Degrees in Culinary
Arts and Gastronomy**   **123**

Studying for Graduate Degrees   124
Graduate Student Recruitment and Registration   128
Induction and Integration of the New Graduate Student   132
Culinary Arts and Gastronomy Graduates and the Future   133

**Chapter 8. Implications of the Introduction of Doctorate
Degrees in Culinary Arts and Gastronomy**   **135**

PhD or ProfD   135
Addressing the Introduction of ProfD Degrees
   in Culinary Arts and Gastronomy   137
Differentiating ProfD from PhD   139
The Nature of Professional Doctoral Study in Culinary
   Arts   140
Process and Product in Doctoral Study   142

Bibliography   **145**

Index   **159**

Acknowledgments

My thanks to the Faculty of Food and Tourism Academic Board and the Sabbatical Leave Committee of Dublin Institute of Technology, who made a sabbatical leave available to me during the year 2001-2002 in the course of which the reflections in the following pages were prepared. Special thanks to all my colleagues in the School of Culinary Arts and Food Technology who bore the weight of this commitment, to Stephen Mennell, Tom Duff, Matt Hussey, Gilles Henegger, Fred Mayo, and John McKenna for their unstinting support, and to Gary McCulloch for his inspiration and persistent encouragement. My thanks also to Otmar Sorgenfrei for his critical observations and advice. However, the sole responsibility for the content of this book is mine.

Introduction

Until very recently, academic qualifications at the undergraduate level in culinary arts and gastronomy were difficult to access, if in fact they existed. The most usual means of obtaining an undergraduate-level qualification in the general field of culinary arts and hospitality was through the path of management degrees in hotel and catering (hospitality). This route has its limits. It raises many issues around education, training, and work in hotels, restaurants, and institutional catering, not least, the development and promotion of vocational education as the means of encouraging "training for hotel and catering work." Its dominant ideology is one of orienting the organization and curricula of hotel and catering schools toward narrow vocational and industry needs. Such task-based training serves only to draw down the intellectual to practice, without understanding.

This book aims to show that in raising culinary arts education to degree level, culinary arts educators, in a particular school, become critically reflective teachers and encourage students to become reflective practitioners free to know, go, do, and be whatever they want to be. Also, it demonstrates that students' futures cannot be limited to teachers' current knowledge on careers available. Students must learn how to learn, to become entrepreneurial innovators, and to lead worthwhile lives as citizens, with a sense of mission and responsibility for the planet and the poor.

Culinary arts and gastronomy education has received little serious scholarly attention to date: (1) because of the lack of theoretical underpinning that would allow it to become a discipline; (2) because of the difficulty in separating the transitory nature and link with physical work, and "industry needs," from those of "education" in the subject, i.e., "science," "art," or "theory," and (3) because of the absence of doctoral programs in the field—a major deficiency in culinary arts education.

1

The academic community concedes that culinary education in its vocational form has limited use in its lower range, that is, it is developed for low-skill, entry-level, task-based technical training for work in kitchens and restaurants. What many, even in the hospitality professional education sector, implicitly deny is that culinary arts and gastronomy has any valid claim as a knowledge field in higher education. Its promoters are seen as callow intruders staking a place in the higher education timetable, justifying their presence on grounds such as pragmatism, persistence, and utility. Culinary arts is a comparatively new area for advanced study in undergraduate education and as such has yet to develop as a subject/discipline with its own appropriate research methodologies. It is an ill-structured knowledge domain which emphasizes the "unfinished" business of action and lacks basic rigor and focus. Nevertheless, this book aims to provide a compelling case for developing graduate professional programs in culinary arts and gastronomy.

In 1995 the first EthnoCulinary Arts Symposium involving participants from Finland, First Nations (Canada), and Ireland took place at the School of Culinary Arts and Food Technology at the Dublin Institute of Technology (DIT). This was followed with a paper presentation by the author at the CHRIE 1996 Conference (Hegarty, 1996) to set out the concept that culinary arts involved developing "chefs into more than mere cooking operatives" (Cullen, 1999).

In 1996 the School of Culinary Arts and Food Technology (formerly the School of Hotel and Catering Operations) adopted a strategy to develop an undergraduate degree in this core subject area. In 1998 a Validation Panel of the Dublin Institute of Technology with two international experts—one from the Culinary Institute of America, the other from the ACCOR Hotel Group—approved the development of the new curriculum integrating vocational and liberal education and validated the four-year undergraduate honors BA in Culinary Arts. In 1999 the Department of Education and Science, following protracted negotiations, sanctioned the running of the BA Culinary Arts as part of the Operational Programme for the DIT.

This sanction affirmed and promoted a change in direction for culinary arts education in Ireland that would ensure its future development as a discipline cognitively, professionally, and in line with the most up-to-date international trends and best practices in the field.

This new curriculum would enable Irish (and other) culinarians to meet the challenges of a multidisciplinary, customer-centered, results-focused, and technology-driven entrepreneurial endeavor, while at the same time incorporating the values of food safety, service quality, customer care, ethics, and passion in the provision of the highest quality food service integral to hospitality and tourism internationally. Thus culinary arts was established as a "discipline" with ties to scholarship in higher education, leading to new opportunities for graduates of culinary arts higher education in the twenty-first century.

In brief, the School of Culinary Arts and Food Technology and the Validation Panel of the Dublin Institute of Technology determined that culinary arts education in Ireland should be an undergraduate-level, four-year honors degree program that would, for the first time, be taught as every subject at the undergraduate level is taught, that is, "in academic alignment." It would optimize career opportunities for people entering the profession at the beginning of the new millennium. The Validation Panel envisaged that students graduating from the four-year honors degree program would become professional culinarians—safe, capable decision makers able to accept personal and professional responsibility, and researchers engaged in improving the knowledge-base and professionalization in the field. Graduates would be flexible, adaptable, reflective researchers and practitioners capable of working in multidisciplinary teams and committed to lifelong learning.

It is hoped that this four-year undergraduate honors degree program incorporating theory and practical knowledge would be generalizable from the School of Culinary Arts and Food Technology to the wider higher education system.

In developing this curriculum, tensions in meeting the alleged requirements for "work" and the accepted criteria for "education" often arose. Such tensions may be expressed in terms of control, as groups representing the food industry competed for involvement and influence with representatives of education. Further, such tensions were likely not to facilitate debate over the kind of curriculum that would incorporate each type of concern. Everyone engaged in the debate on the future of the culinary arts professional education needs to cultivate and espouse the notion of trust. Trust is needed because each participant must be able to rely on others acting as they say they will, and having reciprocity. The tensions and problems encountered in the development of the culinary arts degree highlighted differing ideologies and contrasting beliefs about the purposes of education. Also, much criticism was voiced by the industry over the apparent failure of hotel and catering courses to prepare students more actively for life in the "real world." Formal education and training for hotel and restaurant work has been largely constrained to the preparation of students for entry-level jobs with low-level skills in hotel and catering occupations that, allegedly, improve economic and industry performance.

This book focuses on the story of how a curriculum for a new undergraduate degree in culinary arts was designed, developed, and introduced into a higher education institute of technology. It shows clearly the difficult internal tensions and external constraints experienced in this particular curriculum development. In addition, it considers the steps for establishing graduate degrees in the field. The account is based largely on firsthand observation and documentary analysis using the case study approach. The research focused on the neglected issue of culinary arts education in higher education and on the limitations and possibilities associated with the adoption of a new model of innovation merging liberal and vocational approaches.

Why should we occupy ourselves with the study of culinary arts at the beginning of the twenty-first century? Culinary arts attract contemporary students because of a new realization that cookery not only transforms food but has contributed to the transformation of society (Fernandez-Armesto, 2001, p. 5). Also, interest in the history of food and gastronomy continually attracts contemporary students to study this field. Culinary arts (and hospitality) are important, if neglected, constituents, not only of European social and intellectual life, but also of the quality of human life, globally. From a purely historical point of view the history of culinary arts and hospitality form part of the history of civilization.

Chapter 1

Culinary Arts As a Profession: Possibilities and Prospects

This chapter reflects on issues arising from the development of a liberal/vocational curriculum for an undergraduate degree in culinary arts. Also, it reflects on the possibilities and prospects for establishing culinary arts as a profession with its own graduate programs in higher education.

THE LIBERAL/VOCATIONAL DEBATE IN CULINARY ARTS

The terms "liberal" and "vocational" are often employed to denote two different paradigms in education, two distinct educational philosophies in which the former values knowledge for its own sake, while the latter places a premium on application or on the way knowledge is used in practice. Attempts at exact definitions of either paradigm have tended to prove elusive, although both terms have broad and general connotations and are often found in contexts which seem to be missing from current discourses on curriculum development in the field of culinary arts in particular and hospitality in general.

Alternatively, the terms "liberal" and "vocational" may refer to two educational methodologies, a formal, abstract approach or a concrete, experiential one. At other times, the institutional context determines the consciousness to which the terms "liberal" and "vocational" belong—the kinds of schools, teachers, traditions, and administrative arrangements that are associated with each. These latter arrangements can be compared with the history and traditions of Institutes of Technology in Ireland and the several attempts to develop higher technological (vocational) schools and polytechnic universities elsewhere.

Following many attempts to describe the development of vocational schools in Ireland in the post-1930 period, I suggest that vocational studies in the field of culinary arts never really established a coherent, credible vocational curriculum in their emergence from on-the-job, craft-based apprentice training and practical vocational "needs of industry" base. However, the culinary arts curriculum need not remain constrained and, following Silver's (1983) observation, at this level of discussion it is not so much what is vocational as what are the values and traditions upon which acceptable versions of the vocational could be constructed that matters. If the vocational curriculum is not to continue in the mode of the trivial, transient, and entry-level preparation for low-level jobs typical of traditional professional cookery courses, then the search for the liberal within the vocational curriculum needs to be identified, developed, and broadened—liberating, in a literal sense, both the liberal and vocational potential to become integrated and mutually sustaining. The field of culinary arts education provides ample grounds to explore this potential.

The vocational/liberal topic is not a new one in education. It has been debated as far back as the contrasting educational systems of Sparta and Athens in ancient Greece (Carr, 1993, p. 224; Wellington, 1993). The former was a highly practical, efficient, and state-oriented system while the latter was more creative, individualistic, and humane. According to Carr and Kemmis (1986), the most influential attempt to articulate this view and to differentiate forms of inquiry in terms of their different purposes was Aristotle's threefold classifications of disciplines as "theoretical," "productive," and "practical." Aristotle distinguished between pure knowledge and practical knowledge. Pure knowledge was termed *episteme,* a theoretical, not practical, form of knowledge and a basis for many of the mystical and spiritual movements. Aristotle defined two forms of practical knowledge: *praxis* and *techne.* He suggested that virtue, moral excellence, and righteousness guided praxis. Techne, a term often used for both art and craft, is the kind of knowledge possessed by an expert in one of the specialized crafts. It implies correct action and skill, such as skill in carpentry or cookery. It produces action that accords with an established rule or traditional way of working (Carr and Kemmis, 1986, pp. 33, 34).

This Aristotelian approach to practical knowledge has implications for the development of culinary arts education. Therefore, practical culinary arts education requires a holistic curriculum designed to develop not only technical skills but also the student's individual, intellectual, and moral capabilities. Where such philosophy is missing, an adequate embrace of the kinds of knowing appropriate for the establishment of this new field or discipline is endangered. This distinction in the forms of knowing has implications for culinary arts in undergraduate education, particularly in the role of methods of instruction and the practicum, which heretofore has not been fully examined. For example, little attention has been paid to the difficulty of curriculum material for the student, which is determined by two general factors; the first can be described as the intrinsic complexity of the material, the second is the instructional design or manner in which the material is presented. Traditionally, the culinary practicum has been performed without any requirement for understanding or articulating the cognitive load demanded in the process, or any grasp of the complexity of commensality or the mythology of gastronomy. Inquiry into knowledge production within the field of culinary arts and gastronomy is just beginning to receive some scholarly attention (see Lashley and Morrison, 2000).

It is posited that the absence of an adequate theory of culinary arts learning or of professional education in the field is due primarily to a lack of professional culinary arts education and research at the doctoral level. Nevertheless, it is important to recognize the contribution of practical knowledge in the development of an individual because a culinary arts curriculum that neglects the practical threatens the fundamental core, to understand and engage in the pursuit of happiness for mankind through a gastronomic event, to offer hospitality and appreciate commensality are claimed here to be cognitive achievements leading to an enhanced quality of life through the development of both human intelligence and emotions. To substantiate this claim, however, requires further research in the field of culinary arts and gastronomy.

Since the early twentieth century a notable feature of vocational education has been the tendency to provide curriculum content which is "useful" and "appropriate" to an intended outcome, leading to course programs designed to meet the narrow, restrictive, and constraining needs of industry. The proposition proffered here, influenced largely by the premise that knowledge has an intrinsic value of its own, is that, to substantiate a realistic, relevant, or useful curriculum it is necessary to relate it to human values in an ethical sense, and not just to the immediate demands of market materialism.

RELATIVE IMPORTANCE OF LIBERAL AND VOCATIONAL EDUCATION IN CULINARY ARTS

For the past thirty years the impetus in most Organization for Economic Cooperation and Development (OECD) countries has tended toward the vocationalization of curricula in postcompulsory schooling and the multiplication of vocational training measures designed to bridge the perceived gaps between education provision and social, economic, and industry needs. In more recent times, the impetus has continued because of what Grace (1989) calls the "ideological maneuver," through which the political agenda privileges corporate interests in education while marginalizing others, and many governments seek to use education as a major tool in determining the skill-base of their future workforce for achieving social and economic regeneration. Thus, economic interests dominate the content and process in education and that in turn requires that what counts as knowledge is redefined for practitioners as well as students. Education becomes the acquisition of a mix of skills, and a technical consensus is built around concepts such as efficiency, quality, and accountability. These concepts have been reduced to political slogans and have been deprived of their intellectual engagement and debate. They are expected to be taken to be self-evident, to be self-evidently good, and as a "given" to students and teachers alike (Ozga, 2000, p. 56).

Soucek (1994, pp. 92-93) argues that the formal competencies embedded in economized education provision inspire attitudes that fail to take account of the social consequences of their "rational" approaches to solving social problems. These competencies reflect what he calls a "post-Fordist pedagogy" which treats the development of moral and social attitudes in the same way as it treats instrumental, technical, and mechanical instruction and skill acquisition often mistaken for learning. In such conditions, learners and teachers are denied the opportunity to develop an understanding of specific social problems rather than a temporary achievement of technical competence. Soucek identifies some of the consequences for learners as follows:

> First, it does not provide an opportunity for emotional investment in the learning task. Secondly, the student perceives the task as belonging to someone else; the moral dimension implicit in the task is, therefore, unlikely to be internalized by the student. Finally, the student may not perceive it as a "real" challenge to his or her own capacity to resolve the dilemma creatively and with autonomy. Instead he or she might see it as an exercise in guessing what the teacher thinks is the "right" answer. (Soucek, 1994, p. 97)

This disposition toward constrained discourse in education has implications for culinary arts curriculum development and educational provision at the classroom level, insofar as it predicates the subject matter taught and the type of interaction between students and teachers. In considering culinary arts for higher education there is always a danger of over-balancing, either into its inherent liberal potential at the expense of its practical knowledge and transferable skills or vice versa. Evidence for the latter position can be found in an examination of the rapid development of the National Vocational Qualifications (NVQ) movement in the United Kingdom to the extent that it now outstrips understanding both of its effectiveness and social significance, and more metaphorically, it has become a "colossus skating on rather thin ice" (Gleeson and Hodkinson, 1999, p. 158; Bates, 1999, p. 98). Training, management, and enterprise have become dominant paradigms in the vocational discourse, and educational considerations are often disguised in training terms with the result that the distinction between education and training has become blurred officially (European Commission, 1995). The tension between vocational and liberal education is exacerbated by the tendency to use the term "vocational" almost synonymously and derogatorily with "practical," further alienating it from "academic" as a learning base, when essentially the emphasis should be on a fusion between these two aspects of learning. What we are experiencing in this debate is contradictory discourse within the same strategy.

Undergraduate education in culinary arts aims at providing learning through a practical mode (Mode 2) and therefore to be as liberalizing and humanizing as the traditional liberal approach claims to be. The main change as far as traditional scholarship is concerned is that knowledge production and dissemination—research and teaching—are no longer self-contained activities carried out in the relative isolation of institutions. In this sense, there can be no rational educational basis for a hierarchical distinction between the liberal and the vocational. A technical or technological education which is to have any chance of satisfying the practical needs of the student to lead a worthwhile life must be conceived in a liberal spirit, as a real intellectual enlightenment with regard to principles applied and services rendered. In such an education, geometry and poetry are as essential as turning lathes (Whitehead, 1962, p. 70). It could equally be pointed out that in the reconciled vocational/liberal educational paradigm, turning lathes or making and serving meals are as essential as geometry and poetry.

Vocational education and training are frequently equated by laymen and contrasted by philosophers (Peters, 1966, pp. 32-35) and their definitions are often elusive. However, this relationship needs to be explored if the implications for the curriculum development process of concurring or declining to concur in any shift in the balance between them are to be sufficiently understood. Airey and Tribe (2000, p. 277) have identified the emphasis on the vocational aspects as becoming "a restriction on development." It has tied curriculum development at both undergraduate and graduate levels too closely to the needs of industry (see also Wellington, 1993). This has prevented culinary arts from expanding to deal with the sociological, philosophical, and ethical issues pertaining to the development of the field beyond the task-based instrumentality demanded by industry.

It is evident from Dewey's (1916) attempt to define an educational approach that would combine democratic and humanistic values with science and industry that the main question raised in the debate over vocational education is whether or not democracy is viable under contemporary conditions. Many different criticisms are made of democracy and its education today, but the central issue in the debate over vocational education is whether the conditions of contemporary life, conceived and dominated by materialism, are so defective that a liberal, humane, and democratic society is no longer possible. Wirth (1988, p. 64) tells us that "If we make it," if we "create life-styles which will overcome the divorce of technology from humanistic concerns . . . educational reform and social renewal will go on together." I believe the case would be better stated the other way round; if we engage in educational reform and social renewal then we will create lifestyles that value the human in technological development.

The managerialist and social efficiency adherents in education seem to see the world "steady and whole." They seem to have little understanding and less vision of the purpose of education, and therein lies the limitations of their social and educational theory. The reduction of the debate on the difference between education and training to the "intentions of those who undertake them" raises an outdated dimension and adds little clarity. Nevertheless, at the beginning of the twenty-first century, indications are emerging that traditional distinctions between liberal and vocational education will become more and more irrelevant as the challenge to re-create the citizen in place of the consumer takes on a new dimension. Lawton (1998) reminds us that the young people of the twenty-first century will need a holistic education that reflects the best in both traditions:

> We need to overcome the false and sterile opposition of academic and vocational. Many outside education have complained about this characteristic of educational thinking. Curricula should be designed with a view to eliminating the distinctions between academic and vocational; young people need aspects of both traditions. . . . We need a curriculum which gets beyond thinking in academic and vocational terms. (p. 12)

Clearly, a growing need exists for dialogue between subject historians and curriculum specialists to provide an explanatory basis for the curriculum trying to promote the intellectual development of its students. In the model of subject definition it is often implied that the intellectual discipline is created by a community of scholars, normally, in a university or higher education institution, and is then translated for use as a subject at the earlier stages of education.

Phenix (1964) defines the intellectual discipline base in this way and extends it beyond the university or higher education institute:

> The general test for a discipline is that it should be the character-istic activity of an identifiable organized tradition of men of knowledge, that is of persons who are skilled in certain speci-fied functions that they are able to justify by a set of intelligible standards. (p. 317)

Therefore, an examination of culinary arts as practiced within the habitus of "professional communities" or "communities of profes-sional practice" while necessary, in order to engage with the struggle of culinary arts in its metamorphosis toward a learned form, through the creation of a "community of scholars," may not be sufficient. When the field of culinary arts has been defined, developed, and an undergraduate educational base established for it, it can then be called upon to define, direct, and influence educational and training pro-grams at other levels.

PROFESSIONAL, PROFESSIONALISM, AND PROFESSIONALIZATION IN CULINARY ARTS

A key indicator that a novice in culinary arts has become capable is the development of a professional stance: a set of public behaviors and attributes that recognizes that one shares the abilities and values of one's fellows (Fine, 1996, p. 49; Bourdain, 2001). The technique by which a professional presents himself or herself reveals the presence of enculturation. Professionalism is a stratagem for the display of self, and socialization involves proper display, even if that display blinds one to the economic-instrumental aspects of the occupation. Professionalism in culinary arts has traditionally been defined in terms of workplace competence and standards of performance and practice without regard for the wider sociological, philosophical, and ethical issues such as honesty, food hygiene, and safety, occupational health and safety, justice, and staff and client welfare. Moral responsibility often has been subjugated to the demands of the market, competition, maximizing revenue, and profitability. Thus, practical professional-ism has been reduced to task performance in a manner of technical but unquestioning competency and compliance. The persistence of an unquestioned and unexamined practical knowledge of what culinary arts is remains one of the most serious impediments to improvement in its professional status and raises serious doubts as to whether the occupation can ever become a "profession" at all.

Professionalism is a term applied to how culinary teachers and practitioners actually conduct themselves in practice, not what policymakers or supervisors assert it should be or what others in authority think it ought to be. The aim here is to focus the possibilities and prospects of the development of the culinary arts professionalism from this viewpoint. After all, it is teachers who ultimately hold the key to the success in an educational enterprise as professional practitioners do in a commercial one. Education for culinary arts professionalization and professionalism requires the creation of a "professional" attitude that gives priority to the welfare of clients, is supported by continuous professional self-development, and engages culinary arts teachers and professional practitioners in critical self-reflection and continuous self-improvement.

In this age, professionals have great influence in many areas of our lives. Teachers shape our children's minds. Professors create new generations of professionals. Lawyers handle our disputes. Doctors heal our bodies. All are part of an intricate network of professionals in postmodern society. They often control entry points into positions of power; they certify who is educated and who is uneducated; they determine life and death on the sickbed; they turn the wheels of justice so that some win and some lose. The professionals are in many senses the gatekeepers to success, the wielders of power, and the deciders of right and wrong, truth and beauty. Their claim to knowledge has nowadays become their claim to control. If contemporary society has relinquished much of its power to professionals, it may have done so at its own peril.

That many professionals work more to benefit themselves than to serve their clients is a statistical probability. In many ways, professional groups have become an entrenched, privileged oligarchy that enriches itself at the expense of its clients all the while masking its self-interest under the slogan of "service to the public" or the ethics of "enlightened self-interest." Not only are the motivations of some individual professionals suspect but also many unite in powerful organizations to protect the privileges they have gained.

These professional organizations exhibit a number of unique characteristics. Fundamentally, they are people-centered or people-processing organizations. They recognize that engaging with people as clients, colleagues, shareholders, or managers is not merely a simple technical application, but rather a highly skilled process in which sophisticated judgments match professional decisions concerning the unique contribution of each engagement. Therefore, the first characteristic of professional organizations is that they are highly professionalized, client-centered holistic systems. Further characteristics of professional organizations are that their goals are often both ambiguous and contested. Organizations that are unclear about their goals leave themselves open to manipulation and change of focus by skillful tacticians and politicians. Finally, professional organizations are vulnerable to outside pressures because, often, their clients find themselves to be relatively powerless; in such cases, society generally demands accountability from professionals as a counterbalance to caveat emptor (buyer beware). As a consequence, outsiders demand the right to influence internal professional decisions, and do so, to a greater or lesser extent (Baldridge, 1983, p. 210).

Professionalism then is a situated and contextualized concept, often used as a commonsense way of describing or explaining the work people do. Professionalism is such a positive concept that to dare to question what it means, or to offer a critique of it, sometimes appears impolite (Lawn, 1996, p. 21). The concepts of professionalism and professionalization in culinary arts are problematic because they must be considered in the contexts both of culinary arts learning and of career (professional) practice and teaching. Furthermore, what it means to be professional, to show professionalism, or to pursue professionalization is not universally agreed upon or understood. From a sociological perspective, the contradiction between the claimed status and conditions of work in the culinary profession(s), and the pursuit of ever-grander concoctions and culinary edifices as a means of improving these, remains into the present day. Yet, the significance of how individual cooks with exceptional skills and creative abilities rise to particular eminence and enjoy the fruits of success has not been an area of any serious study. This omission needs to be addressed by gaining information on professional practice if culinary arts is to become a profession, improve its social ranking and pecuniary rewards, and emulate the old "liberal professions" such as law and medicine. The likelihood of any kind of professionalization being achieved and having effect through curriculum development is a function of the subject development, where the selection of subject matter is determined in large measure by the judgment and practices of specialist scholars who lead inquiries in the field (Layton, 1972, in Goodson, 1998). Who produces this knowledge, what is produced, why it is produced, and where it is produced need to be conceptualized, described, understood, and evaluated. Further research is required in order to establish the meaning of a "subject community" in culinary arts that, in turn, would lead to a "community of professional practitioners" enabled to reflect on their practice, engage with the research, and build toward professionalism. The end game would be the creation of a "community of scholars," that is, students and teachers, engaged in research and publication, developing the disciplines of culinary arts.

Many occupations in the twentieth century have sought to professionalize themselves by laying claim to a systematic body of knowledge acquired through specialized training, an ethic of service to the public, and a measure of autonomous authority in its particular field. Nowadays, such claims are seemingly idealistic in increasingly market-oriented occupations like culinary arts. Nevertheless, the client-centered strategy of the new approach offers culinary arts education the potential for professionalization.

Important distinctions between professionalization as a social and political project or mission designed to enhance the interests of an occupational group, and professionalism as something which defines and articulates the quality and character of people's actions within that group have been drawn. Current debates about professionalism, professional, and professionalization carry different connotations of what it means to be professional. Hargreaves and Goodson (1996, pp. 4-19) examine six different and often overlapping discourses that they call classical professionalism, flexible professionalism, practical professionalism, extended professionalism, complex professionalism, and postmodern professionalism to determine how these advance the cause of professionalization and whether this is a good thing.

The notion that professionalism in culinary arts education should be guided, not only by interests of commercialism or self-serving status enhancement, or confined to matters of technical competence, but by ethical and sociopolitical visions and purposes, and personal, practical reflection about how best to become a reflective practitioner and deliver professional practice as defined by the community of scholars rather than by bureaucratic others, is presented as an ideal model for moving forward.

FOUR ESSENTIAL CRITERIA FOR DISTINGUISHING PROFESSIONAL OCCUPATIONS

Carr and Kemmis (1986, pp. 7-8), among others, provide a set of four essential criteria used traditionally for distinguishing professional from nonprofessional occupations. The first is that the "methods and procedures" of professionals are underpinned by a "body of theoretical knowledge." The second criterion is that professionals are deeply committed to "the well-being of their clients." Third, for an occupation to be truly professional, practitioners must be free from external pressure in their dealings with clients. Therefore, a significant degree of autonomy is necessary. Fourth, a true profession must have the right to determine the sorts of policies, organization, and procedures that should govern the profession as a whole. This places the responsibility for his or her own professional development onto the individual practitioner or educator.

The new discourse in culinary arts higher education seems to reject the notion of culinary arts educators as dedicated professionals applying their specialist and complex knowledge to further the well-being of their students. Instead, it seems to depict them as untrustworthy, self-interested individuals, motivated by extrinsic rewards, in need of control, regulation, and management. Clearly, it is a triumph of hope over experience to expect that such self-interested, untrustworthy individuals would combine to contribute to the achievement of educational quality assurance, effectively and efficiently implemented in the institutes of education where they work. There is also some danger when such a group of people are treated as unreliable; they are, thereby, given common ground upon which to take a stand and this sometimes encourages them to defend the indefensible. Culinary arts lecturers having as their spokespersons strong trade unions, rather than professional associations do not, it is suggested, have the same "voice" in shaping how their status as professionals may be gained. When lecturers are treated as employees rather than professional academics, in turn they respond in predictable fashion, and not as, say, the Medical Association, the Law Society, or the Chartered Institute of whatever, do. Such associations or societies are not merely the guardians of their corpus of knowledge and professional status; they negotiate and lobby with government and have access to media, so that government seeking to pass legislation, in the teeth of these professional bodies' objections, would find itself in public conflict. Culinary lecturers are not yet in such a position. As long as they continue to resort to the language and tactics of industrial action, professional standing will elude them (Hutton, 2001, p. 26).

Chapter 2

Culinary Arts Curriculum Development: The Heart of the Educational Enterprise

Curriculum design, development, and delivery are at the heart of the educational enterprise. The principal educational function of higher education institutions, individually or collectively, is to design and plan, to prepare and deliver, and assess and examine the curriculum and its outputs in ways that foster and support student learning (OECD, 1998, p. 55). It is also an important point of observation for inquiry into the nature of lecturers' professional credibility, in terms of claims to subject authority in the field, including public acknowledgment that the subjects they teach are professional within a recognized profession (Helsby and McCulloch, 1996, p. 56).

Reflection on one particular curriculum development process for an undergraduate degree in culinary arts and the prospects and potential for its further development to master's and doctoral levels, begins with a recognition that the curriculum is constructed for a number of purposes, including an innate desire for ordered knowledge. Such a curriculum should embrace the knowledge fields of arts, business, science, and technology, the ability to make things (in this case, the meal experience), incorporate an understanding of the industry, and lead to the validation of the bachelor's, master's, and the doctorate in culinary arts. Also, it examines the contribution of the curriculum development process to establishing the educational and cultural capital necessary to develop culinary arts as a subject suitable for advanced scholarship in higher education.

TOWARD A DEFINITION OF CURRICULUM

"Curriculum" is a difficult term to define exactly; it has a high level of generality and a low level of precision. "Curriculum" derives from the Latin *currere* and originally meant a running track for athletes. This derivation conjures up many images that continue to be popularly associated with curriculum—marking out the course to be run, clearly showing the start and the finish, sorting out competitors into some kind of running order, drawing up a program of events, and finally offering various laurels to those who emerge as winners. This definition of curriculum is insufficient for, as Eggleston (1977) suggests, the curriculum is concerned with the presentation of knowledge, and it involves a pattern of learning experiences, both instrumental and expressive, designed to enable it to be engaged by the students within the educational institution. It is a formal arrangement for the pursuit of education. The term "curriculum" is usually associated with the subjects or courses taught at the secondary and undergraduate levels. Sometimes it is applied to the subject syllabus, at other times it is used in respect to the collection of subjects (programs/disciplines) taught.

Criticism of the "field of curriculum, that it was moribund and unable by its present methods and principles to . . . contribute to the advancement of education" had impact (Schwab, 1969, p. 1). Following this criticism there was a significant reappraisal of curriculum theory. Barrow (1984, p. 40) argued for a movement away from models in favor of a more flexible approach. Pratt (1980, p. 10) tells us that the curriculum developer must allow for consideration of values outside the immediate area of the subject, and of the values of society. MacDonald (1977, p. 12) suggests that there are three critical activities inherent in curriculum development: (1) talk about the curriculum; (2) talk about praxis (planning talk), and (3) praxis (action). These ideas have immense implications for reflection on culinary arts curriculum development because the actual curriculum development occurred in "learning by doing" rather than in a purely theoretical framework. The theorists offered benchmarks against which to interpret what was really going on in developing a culinary arts curriculum.

CURRICULUM DEVELOPMENT—THE PROCESS

Following a 1996 review of the Quality Assurance Procedures that enabled the Dublin Institute of Technology to award its own degrees, the school had a unique opportunity to design a new curriculum from scratch. Some of the first questions were "Where do we begin the development of a new curriculum? What are the trigger mechanisms for the development of a new curriculum? What needs to be done and by whom in order to develop a new course?" Clearly, there were many different responses to these questions and different ways of conceptualizing and framing a culinary arts curriculum.

A variety of possible responses faced the school in its approach to framing this curriculum. One such response was to base the design of learning outcomes and the prescription of learning objectives on occupation or job analysis, that is, examining jobs actually carried out by people at work. The benefit of such an approach was that it depended not on what someone in authority thought should be done or what ideally ought to be done, but on what people at work actually did. Another was to trace the various approaches to curriculum development exemplified in the work of people such as Bobbitt (1918), Tyler (1949), and Bloom, Krathwohl, and Masia (1956), who dominated curriculum theory until relatively recently. Stenhouse (1989, p. 85) advocated a process approach to curriculum development in an attempt to provide an alternative to the traditional models. The curriculum process being reflected upon in this book is for a new course— an undergraduate degree in culinary arts—that came into being for a variety of reasons related to school survival in a situation of institutional change, unmet demands from students for the opportunity to better themselves, and the need to create a higher education dimension for a culinary arts program where none previously existed. A framework for addressing the questions derived from a comprehensive study of curriculum theory is illustrated in Figure 2.1. However, useful as this linear flow chart for a curriculum development process illustration is, it does not convey the dynamics of a process that is iterative, emotional, and holistic with many actions occurring together in the form of a multiple helix.

The process began with collecting and analyzing information on what might be taught, and in determining the beliefs and values of the curriculum development team in relation to the broad goals of the curriculum. These answers in turn contributed to the decisions on aims and objectives, content and structure, and methods of student assessment and examination.

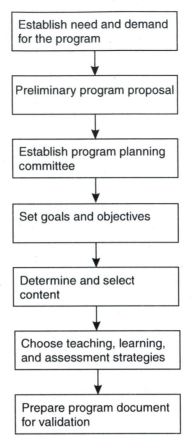

FIGURE 2.1. Curriculum Development Process (*Source:* Toohey, 1999.)

Composition of a Curriculum Development Team

The practical application of the theoretical framework for curriculum development necessitated

- forming a curriculum team,
- electing or appointing a chairperson and secretary,
- defining the curriculum project brief/preliminary program proposal,

- electing or selecting the curriculum development team,
- establishing wider stakeholder support,
- preparing the aims and objectives of the program,
- selecting content of the program,
- determining teaching and learning strategies, and
- assessing methods to be engaged at an early stage.

The academic level of the curriculum would challenge the composition and size of the curriculum team. The nature of their academic qualifications, their interpersonal relations, and the time available for them to work together influences the size of the team. At one extreme everybody is involved—all of the teaching staff, representatives of industry, government agencies, and other interested parties. At the other extreme, only those sufficiently interested to do the work are involved.

The size and configuration of a team developing a curriculum for a one year top-up program will vary from that of a team developing or reviewing a two-year certificate program, a four-year undergraduate, or a graduate degree program. Where an entirely new course is to be developed, the knowledge input from the team is expected to be significant and the team membership should reflect this. Scott (1999) advised, in his work on change in vocational education, that the key criteria for selecting members of the team are first, that they see the innovation as being desirable and aspire to achieve it, and second, that they have the skills to make it work.

Appointing a suitable chairperson and secretary is of paramount importance in contributing to the successful outcome of the curriculum development process. The chairperson should be able to create an atmosphere where all the issues will be discussed and clarified while keeping the process in line with the school's educational objectives. The role of the chairperson is to keep the bigger, broader picture in view, to enhance understanding of issues, and raise the level of discussion, debate, and interaction. The secretary's role is normally that of maintaining an accurate record of all proceedings, allowing for contributions to be recorded and retained as part of the text of the project and assisting absentees from meetings in accessing the curriculum development story.

Prior to selecting team members, it is recommended that a project brief or preliminary program proposal be prepared defining the nature of the curriculum and its aims. This is required in order to develop a cohesive approach for the curriculum development, to ensure that an overview of what is required can be clearly established, and to enable team members, appropriate to the project, to be selected. The project brief should provide for a level of flexibility so the course of development opportunities may be identified, proven attractive, and taken up. Once the preliminary course proposal is established, the team members emerge according to their expertise in the areas of the subject knowledge, curriculum design, pedagogy, measurement and assessment, organization, and writing skills. It is important to generate "ownership" of the project by as many stakeholders as possible, because individual teachers, industry practitioners, and professional associations not consulted for their views often feel left out and could choose to resist, opt out, or obstruct the development.

Organization for Team Dynamics

In order to create an atmosphere of seriousness and to organize a systematic and consistent approach to the project's group dynamics, Norton (1985, pp. 14, 15) specified a number of features required to accommodate and facilitate this interaction; meeting times should be agreed in advance to facilitate all members, a suitable and fixed meeting place should be decided which is free from distraction, and refreshments should be provided.

The range of people whose input and advice can be extremely useful when establishing a curriculum development project include academic and administrative staff and other specialist staff. These include educational specialists, leaders at the cutting edge of the discipline, representatives of professional associations, students, and graduates. Pratt (1980) suggests that opinions should be sought from three categories of people, namely, those who have a right to be consulted, those whom it is politically expedient to consult, and those who have particular insights or expertise. This strategy would facilitate wider awareness through stakeholder and staff room talk, and in addition, could help to promote some level of enthusiasm and input in the project. By inviting academic and industry participation in the curriculum development project, the commitment of the wider stakeholder group is accommodated and the potential for wider "ownership" increased.

Establishing Aims and Objectives

Educational aims are the basis for curriculum objectives. Aims are broad statements of intent while objectives are specific targets (Nicholls and Nicholls, 1978, p. 38). The idea of formulating objectives which would identify what students are intended to achieve, as the basis for curriculum design was first put forward by Tyler (1949):

> If an educational program is to be planned and if efforts for continued improvements are to be made, it is very necessary to have some conception of the goals that are being aimed at. These educational objectives become the criteria by which material are selected, content is outlined, instructional procedures are developed and tests and examinations are prepared. (p. 3)

The overall aim of the curriculum has significant implications for the development process, insofar as it sets the context and the vision for the development and provides focus for the curriculum team. The aim, based on a rationale or philosophy or justification of the proposed curriculum, defines and selects the parameters and helps to define the nature of the curriculum.

The aim of a curriculum leading to the award of a degree is likely to signify at least three kinds of achievement according to the Higher Education Quality Council (HEQC) (1997). HEQC characterizes these aims as follows:

- *Field-specific knowledge*—the possession of a body of knowledge and other qualities particular to the field (or fields) studied
- *Shared attributes*—the possession of certain more general attributes that might be common to graduates from families of degrees, whether associated with cognate matter and/or approach (such as the life sciences or the performing arts)
- *Generic attributes*—the possession of yet more general attributes which might be common to all or most graduates (HEQC, 1997)

The goals teachers have for graduates of their programs are similar and very close to the lists put out by HEQC. Toohey (1999) lists an example of what one group of university lecturers said they wanted to achieve with respect to their students, through their teaching:

- understand that knowledge is not fixed and that they can contribute to it;
- think, question, and challenge;
- solve problems both familiar and unfamiliar;
- make informed choices;
- have a rich cultural and intellectual life;
- be critical and question their surroundings;
- be aware of their own values and beliefs in dealing with other people;
- treat others humanely;
- be able to interpret and evaluate research findings;
- be able to analyze increasingly complex problems and to work on increasingly better thought out answers;
- be able to communicate effectively in all ways;
- be able to integrate personal experience and theory;
- work efficiently, effectively, and safely;
- act with confidence and integrity;
- have acquired the knowledge base of the discipline; and
- continuously seek out knowledge (pp. 71, 72).

She also suggests that curriculum development teams develop program goals. Choices about which goals to pursue are out of the realm of individual decision making and are opened up for team examination and critique. If staff can agree to work on developing the same set of attributes throughout the program, the impact of their efforts will be increased. Toohey (1999) goes on to tell us that some of the most interesting higher education programs in the past decade have been focused around a limited number of core attributes which are consciously developed through all stages of the program. Such an approach has the advantage of keeping attention on a limited, and therefore memorable, number of goals. It allows these attributes and skills to be developed in a coherent way over the duration of the program so that students can move from simple understandings to more complex ones. Also, aims and objectives influence content. Aims and objectives need to focus on the big questions of curriculum development, and to help lecturers account for their work in the context of the scrutiny of the stakeholders and managerialists. Learning objectives serve as statements to help evaluate the achievement of students in relation to them. They serve to convey the intentions of the curriculum developers to students and the wider market of stakeholders. A curriculum organized around a commitment to cognitive structures will present many examples of key concepts so that students can establish what the essential elements are by comparison and contrast. Last, it requires that all lecturers in the program accept responsibility for developing these attributes in the context of an integrated curriculum. It does not allow them to get lost in the drive simply to master content and technical skills. Once the overall aim has been identified, learning objectives or outcomes should be established to reinforce this aim.

In the traditional craft-based, apprentice vocational training in culinary arts, the emphasis has been on instrumental task (or task-element) performance, with heavy reliance on behavioral or instructional objectives delivered in a didactic form to demonstrate unspecified competence(s). Among the most persistent critics of the competence approach are Gleeson and Hodkinson (1999), Bates and Dunston (1995), Bates (1999), and Hyland (1994). Gleeson and Hodkinson (1999, p. 158), following a review of numerous studies, point out that such education and training lags behind equivalent systems in most developed countries, and that there is a consensus that vocational training provision has not worked, either for a majority of young school leavers, or in meeting the perceived needs for a better workforce. Bates (1999, p. 112) criticizes competence-based education on the grounds that it runs counter to the "spirit of education." She emphasizes the importance of the individual in the construction of meanings, and the need for education to treat learning as a creative process in which the outcomes are, to some extent, unpredictable. Hyland (1994, p. 235) argues that competence-based education atomizes and fragments learning into measurable chunks, rather than creating a valuing process and experience. It is concerned only with performance outcomes, and, most important, instead of encouraging critical reflection on alternative perspectives it offers a monocultural view based on the satisfaction of narrow performance criteria directed toward fixed and predetermined ends. In culinary arts, the competence-based curriculum has come to be regarded as mechanistic and reductionist, and unlikely to foster the fullest possible potential of human development. For an undergraduate curriculum in culinary arts, the emphasis needs to be placed on recognizing and fostering the intellectual development of the students.

Structure of the Curriculum and Content Selection

The traditional way of specifying curriculum content is through the medium of subjects. These can be understood from two major perspectives: the historical and the philosophical. Much of the research for developing a social history of knowledge owes a debt to the work of critical theorists and sociologists of knowledge from the 1960s onward (Goodson, 1998, p. 6). In the 1960s, a new impetus to scholarship on subjects came from sociologists, especially sociologists of knowledge. Musgrove (1968, p. 101) urges researchers to:

> Examine subjects both within the [academy] and the nation at large as social systems sustained by communication networks, material endowments and ideologies. Within a school and within a wider society subjects as communities of people, competing and collaborating with one another, defining and defending their boundaries, demanding allegiance from their members and conferring a sense of identity upon them . . . even innovation which appears to be essentially intellectual in character can usefully be examined as the outcome of social interaction.

The second school of explanation is essentially philosophical. It precedes and stands in contradiction to sociological perspectives. The philosophical perspective is well summarized in the work of Hirst (1965):

> No matter what the ability of the [student] may be, the heart of all his development as a rational being is, I am saying, intellectual. Maybe we shall need very special methods to achieve this development in some cases. Maybe we still have to find the best methods for the majority of the people. But let us never lose sight of the intellectual aim upon which so much else, nearly ev-

erything else, depends. Secondly, it seems to me that we must get away completely from the idea that linguistic and abstract forms of thought are not for some people.

However, these frameworks are not mutually exclusive, nor are they the only way of specifying curriculum content in learning situations that demand the multifaceted approach of the culinary arts curriculum.

In culinary arts vocational training, competent performance may be conceived in terms of ability to perform specific kitchen tasks but in undergraduate education it needs to be conceptualized far more broadly. The roles that a culinarian undertakes may be identified as those of knowledgeable and creative practitioner (providing both nutrition and gastronomic pleasure), connoisseur, manager, professional leader, communicator, and educator. Once defined, the cognitive curriculum is chosen for the opportunities it provides for mastering important concepts, language, and practicing key intellectual abilities.

One approach to definition is that roles may be analyzed to determine what knowledge, skills, attributes, and dispositions students will need to acquire in order to be able to perform them. Knowledge and skills may be sequenced to ensure an advanced, complex, and sophisticated final performance. A danger of this method of curriculum development is that it relies overly on task analysis or task competence, unlikely to foster the fullest possible potential for individual development.

Stenhouse (1989, p. 87) argues that it is possible to select curriculum content without reference to ends of any kind other than representing the form of knowledge in the curriculum. Thus, the competition between content and skills is eliminated because concepts and skills are both contextualized in reasoning, reflecting, problem solving, and in critical thinking. Content should be selected to exemplify the most important processes, the key concepts, the areas and situations in which criteria hold. In a quotation that powerfully acknowledges the difficulties of curriculum development, he recommends that the focus be on "speculation rather than mastery." This connects with the Aristotelian view of knowledge. The process is not predictive. It does not specify outcomes and is not controllable. Key procedures, concepts, and criteria in culinary arts need to become the focus of speculation as well as mastery.

RECOGNIZING THE MASTER PERFORMER

One way of getting at these key core attributes is through the concept of master performer (Toohey, 1999, pp. 73-74). This idea of a master performer can be used not just for analyzing purely vocational task-based roles, but in any discipline—philosopher, historian, economist, physicist, choreographer, physician, and so forth. Sometimes it is possible to recognize real role models, but more often curriculum developers are likely to envisage a composite performer, an imaginary figure who exemplifies the kinds of skills and knowledge, values and attributes that are characteristic of an educated person—or perhaps an accomplished performer. In thinking about what constitutes this kind of performance the curriculum developers need to ask certain questions: What roles do master performers assume? What distinguishes excellent performers from the merely average? The outcomes of exercises like the analysis of the master performer and the desired qualities of graduates need to be formulated into the general aims or goals for the program of study by the curriculum team. These will be useful if they positively influence teaching and learning strategies during curriculum implementation. Negative influences arise when those who come later to teach in the program have not shared the experience of formulating the aims and/or goals for the program.

CURRICULUM DESIGN FOR DEEP LEARNING

To create conditions suitable for deep learning, i.e., the right motivational context, the appropriate activities for learning, the opportunity to interact with others and to build one's own well-structured knowledge base, can become a challenge for the curriculum developer. The factors which enable deep learning must be built into the curriculum at the development and design stage. If they are not, individual lecturers, however creative they may be, will always be struggling to overcome the structural limitations of the program. If, for example, the content to be covered is too broad, the assessment requirements too narrow and prescriptive, and the teaching methods too confined by timetabling, class numbers, or accommodation restrictions, it would be very difficult to create an environment within which students really engage with the subject. This reflection on the curriculum development process, constrained by traditional and procedural rubrics, necessitates, on the part of the lecturer, a willingness to deconstruct and the capability to reconstruct the subject, in the pursuit of academic legitimacy.

Culinary arts education may be viewed, in this first stage of its development, as a callow intruder, staking its place on the undergraduate timetable, justifying its presence on grounds such as persistence and utility. Learners become attracted to the subject because of its bearing on matters of concern to them (jobs). The lecturers are rarely trained specialists, but bring to their task the missionary enthusiasm of pioneers. The dominant criterion is relevance to the needs and interests of the industry rather than the needs and interests of the learners (Layton, 1972).

My own sense is that culinary arts education is metamorphosing toward a position of scholarly activity, emerging along with a core of highly educated specialists from which new lecturers can be recruited. Students are still likely to be attracted to the field, as much by its reputation and academic status as by its relevance to their own problems and concerns. The evolution of an internal logic and rigorous discipline in the subject is becoming increasingly influential on the selection and organization of course content (see Weiss, 1994).

The final stage of culinary arts education's development is, it is suggested, still some way away. When it arrives, its educators and professional practitioners will constitute the "professional body" with established "rules and values" fulfilling four essential criteria, by which a profession may be recognized. The study of the knowledge content of culinary arts should then move beyond the ahistorical process of "management" analysis toward a metaphysics of cuisine and a detailed anthropological and historical investigation of the motives and actions behind these subjects and disciplines. A number of examples such as geography, rural studies, and biology offer researchers in this field opportunities for guidance.

Layton's example for "becoming a subject," although taken from secondary school subjects rather than from undergraduate education, is not considered problematic for curriculum development in culinary arts for two reasons. First, because the culinary arts curriculum metamorphosing from a second-level vocational training base to an undergraduate academic platform could be said to mirror the first stage of Layton's model. Second, it seemed to me to be a very user-friendly model. Subjects and disciplines, far from being timeless monolithic statements of intrinsically worthwhile content are, according to Goodson (1981, p. 167), in constant flux. It is not unreasonable, therefore, that the study of culinary arts knowledge should tend in its redefinition as a subject and a discipline toward the liberal end of the vocational/liberal continuum. Goodson's assertion that content, subjects, and disciplines may be in constant flux does not mean that their intrinsic value is diminished. Intrinsic worthwhile content needs to be based on sound educational values.

The definition of a subject is always problematic, and this is especially true of one that has a variety of continuously changing contexts. The attempt to benchmark deep learning for master performer focuses on what might be expected of a student following undergraduate or graduate studies in an institute of higher education. Attention must be paid to a comprehensive view of the subject in terms of knowledge, understanding, application, analysis, synthesis, and reflection incorporating advanced research skills.

ASSESSMENT AND EXAMINATION
OF DIFFERENT KINDS OF LEARNING

The curriculum framework includes the goals, aims, and objectives set down for the program and because assessment drives the curriculum, it is reasonable to assume that these would be developed through content and assessed throughout the program. Curriculum and assessment development should be undertaken together with planned coherence, for assessment is the tail that wags the curriculum dog. Many teachers espouse goals of critical thinking and logical argument involving selection and use of relevant evidence, systematic problem-solving, and self-directed learning, but far too frequently their assessments do not evidence any of these, instead students are permitted to pass by replaying information provided in lecture notes, drilled practice, and prescribed textbook readings. In such situations, the examination and assessment system will be a far less powerful influence on the approach students take than the expressed goals. Students quickly learn that whatever the lecturer says, a surface approach to learning will suffice to achieve a pass in a particular subject. Those who continue to take a deep approach are not necessarily advantaged under this kind of assessment system. Four general questions arise, namely, What have students learned? What has the curriculum contributed to their learning? How can this information improve the curriculum? and How can it point to new directions for the development of culinary arts in higher education?

Underpinning these questions lies the more fundamental question, What should students learn? This question must be addressed if assessment instruments are to be designed which are consistent with the mission and practice of the program and with the demands of the students' personal and professional life, family, and the world of work. When thinking about the different kinds of knowledge, understanding, skills, and personal attributes which could or should be assessed as part of a degree program it may be beneficial to look at Habermas's (1972) construct of three different kinds of human interests which result in distinctly different kinds of knowledge or understanding:

1. The interest in control or mastery of one's environment, leading to the development of technical, empirical, or conventional knowledge.
2. The interest in developing shared understanding with others and communicating and negotiating meaning, leading to interpretative or hermeneutic knowledge.
3. The interest in freedom—freedom from unthinking acceptance of social and political systems and individual limitations—leading to the development of self-reflective and critical understandings.

The characteristics of each of these different kinds of knowledge imply distinctly different kinds of assessment. The distinguishing feature of technical, empirical, or conventional knowledge is that it is the object of general agreement and acceptance. Rules, formulae, vocabulary, and procedures all represent codified and established knowledge. The weighting given to technical knowledge and the extent to which such knowledge is believed to be worth assessing will depend on the nature of the discipline and on what is valued by the curriculum development team in the context of the wider academic community. Toohey (1999) informs us that the way in which assessment in higher education is conceived has changed significantly over the past twenty years. She cites Mentkowski et al. (1991) as follows:

> Lately . . . I've . . . begun to identify some of the educational assumptions that are beginning to drive higher educational assessment more broadly. I can see three intertwined but distinct aspects: First, expanding the outcomes of college to include not only what students know but also what they are able to do has led to the development of alternative assessments including performance and portfolio assessment. Second, expanding learning to include collaboration with others and more reflective and self-sustaining learning, has led to assessment projects produced by groups of students and to more attention to self-assessment. Third, expanding educational goals to include personal growth has led to assessment of broad developmental patterns over time. (Mentkowski et al., 1991, p. 13)

There are at least two reasons for asserting that mechanisms to ensure formative reflection and feedback on skills acquisition, both in practicum and on professional internship, need to be developed in such a way as to achieve some equivalence in weighting for all subjects in a program. First, assessment can be a vital link between curriculum and teaching through providing feedback to the students, teachers, parents, and other interested parties (stakeholders), and second, it can place significantly more power and responsibility in the hands of the learners themselves (Lawton, 1996). Assessments, in this sense, should be curriculum-driven instead of, as is often the case, examination dominated. The results of an examination-led curriculum are predictable, what tends to get taught is what is examinable, but what is most examinable is often of least importance. The process of teaching to the test, evidenced in the approach of some teachers of professional cookery and other courses, inhibits learning and understanding and contributes to simple rote learning of prescribed texts. There is a need therefore to move away from the examinations' culture described, to one more conducive to creative learning and teaching. Also, there is a need to understand that educational standards are not raised by assessment and examinations whether tough or easy, but by improving the quality of teaching and learning and what goes on in the school (the hidden curriculum).

There has been a paradigm shift in assessment in the recent past— a shift toward assessing understanding and meaning rather than rote learning and recall of information. This implies a move from an examination-as-hurdle model (where proof of quality is in the numbers that fail) to an assessment model which tries to elicit the students' best performance. The key aspects of such a model are

- a range of assessment activities, offering a wide opportunity for students to achieve;
- a match between assessment and classroom practice;
- an extended interaction between student and lecturer to explain the assessment requirement;
- normal classroom setting, which is therefore not unduly threatening; and
- a range of response modes other than written (Gipps, 1994).

This assessment model lends itself particularly well to curriculum development in undergraduate vocational/liberal education programs where the professionalization of culinary arts offers a context for its application.

Chapter 3

Framework for the Development and Validation of a New Culinary Arts Degree Program

The assurance of the educational quality in a culinary arts program begins with the initial curriculum proposal leading to eventual validation or accreditation. This chapter sets the framework for the culinary arts curriculum journey described in detail in Chapter 6, in its evolution from a traditional craft-based vocational training paradigm with its own modes of thinking, to a new paradigm created in culinary arts (and gastronomic) inquiry, which would be different and lead to the provision of a new integrated undergraduate degree curriculum. This chapter and the next lean heavily on my experiences as member of the DIT Quality Assurance Steering Committee and on two publications: the Dublin Institute of Technology's *Quality Assurance Handbook* (1995, 1997), and Duff et al. (2000a) *Academic Quality Assurance in Irish Higher Education,* both of which are justly famous.

CULINARY ARTS PROGRAM CONCEPTION

The curriculum journey leading to a BA in Culinary Arts began formally on May 29, 1996, at an inaugural meeting of all staff in the school. The meeting was convened to propose action on curriculum development in the light of changes in the institute, the merging of six independent colleges into one institute, pursuing university status, and the mechanisms that identified a demand for such development.

Five mechanisms were identified as triggers prompting the development of the new culinary arts curriculum. The first was increasing numbers of students remaining in full-time education and training after the end of their compulsory requirement seeking to climb the progression ladder, whereby they could progress via undergraduate education to a university degree (Trant et al., 1999). Experience elsewhere led to a consensus that current vocational education and training provision has not worked either for the majority of school leavers or for the perceived need for a better workforce (Gleeson and Hodkinson, 1999). The proposed new culinary arts curriculum aimed to "do something" about these issues in an Irish, and where feasible, international context. The second trigger mechanism influencing the development of the new curriculum was the reconfiguration of courses in the hotel management program (a sister program in the college) that reduced the service-teaching provision from the school by 24 percent. This adversely affected the status of the school and career opportunities for the staff. Traditionally, approximately half of the school's work comprised teaching theory and practical cookery and restaurant operations in the hotel management diploma and degree programs. A third trigger was the demand by graduates of the two-year Certificate in Culinary Arts for higher level educational opportunities for them to "better" themselves (McMahon, 2000). The fourth trigger mechanism was the gap identified in the training and education provision for head chefs and the capability requirements of their positions (Erraught, 1998). The fifth comprised developments within the institute, seeking to amalgamate six independently autonomous specialist colleges into one Institute of Technology, pursuing its own degree awarding powers, and seeking university status. Also, there was an unarticulated interest in curriculum development within the school, which was the matter of informal conversation for many years and which came to fruition in the complexity of circumstances which existed in the school in 1996.

Sources of motivation for the development of the program proposal came from: the inspiration of the experiences and observations of the lecturers in the discipline; changes occurring in the discipline; changes occurring in the Institute, faculty, and school, and the developing of a corpus of professional knowledge. Ideas for the program arose from individual research activities and experiences of lecturers with food service industries, restaurant and hotel businesses, and contract catering.

THE PRELIMINARY PROGRAM PROPOSAL

In order to begin the curriculum development process, a preliminary program proposal or curriculum project brief was formulated for discussion within the school, and presented at the Faculty Academic Board. This preliminary program proposal detailed the following fundamental aspects of the program:

- Title and academic award sought
- Support for the program from industry/commerce, government agencies, etc.
- Associated professional bodies and their involvement/support
- Market demand, both by industry for graduates with the range of knowledge and skills to be acquired in the program, and by potential students
- Relevance of the new program to the mission and strategic plan of the institution and of the departments and faculty concerned, its impact on courses and programs currently offerred, and on the human and physical resources available
- Program philosophy and aims
- Objectives, value to be added to students by program
- Mode of delivery (full-time, part-time, modularized, other) and duration
- Methods of teaching/learning/examination envisaged
- Numbers of students planned over an initial five-year period
- Academic entry requirements for the first year
- Student transfer arrangements from other programs/institutions into later years of the program, including recognition of prior experiential learning
- Industrial or other links, including possible professional internships
- Main subjects, their relative contributions in each year, and the integration of the program elements
- Class contact hours in each year (lectures, practical/studio, tutorial, others)
- Student workload in each year
- Accommodations available and required in each year
- Equipment and resources available and required in each year

- Academic staff available and additional staff required in each year
- Full-time staff recruitment required and time scale for their recruitment
- Technical support staff available and additional staff required
- Administrative staff available and additional staff required
- Staff development required to run/develop the program (DIT Course Quality Assurance Handbook, 1995, 1997; Duff et al., 2000a)

The formulation of the preliminary program proposal required substantial work input by the staff members proposing the program. The process involved iterative discussions and feedback with colleagues, head of school and institute directorate, as well as with industry. The preliminary program proposal aimed at constructing a persuasive case to the authorities of the Institute and to the Department of Education for the allocation of the resources—personnel, accommodation, and equipment—necessary to ensure delivery of the program over the planned duration.

Consideration of the Preliminary Program Proposal by the Institute Directorate

At each academic and administrative level of quality assurance within the institute, the preliminary program proposal was evaluated in terms of both its academic aspects and the resources required to deliver it. These aspects were viewed in the context of the Institute's policy priorities, available resources, and resources to be acquired. Thus, the school needed to consider the feasibility of the proposal, including its impact on other programs and activities and how it might affect the balance of provision and the priorities of the school and faculty.

The primary role of the discussions with the directorate, at an early stage, was to ensure that the proposal was consistent with the policy and development plan of the Institute, and that adequate resources would be made available to deliver it. The directorate advised the school of its decision to support the proposal and of their conditions attaching to its approval.

PREPARATION OF THE PROGRAM DOCUMENTATION

Following the approval of the preliminary program proposal, outline planning permission for the program was granted. This allowed the proposing curriculum team to proceed to design and develop and draft the program documentation required for the validation process. However, a caveat existed; the outline planning permission for the program was no guarantee that the proposed program would be validated or, if it was, that the program would be offered in any particular year.

In drafting the program documentation, the curriculum team drew upon a wide range of expertise both within and outside the school and faculty involved and the Institute as a whole, and called on external expertise as required.

For ease of processing and evaluation, the Institute's quality assurance handbook advises that it is desirable for the curriculum team to provide a structured self-evaluation in the documentation required for the validation process. Although there are many different formats for preparing such documentation, Duff et al. (2000a, pp. 66-67) recommend that it include at least the following two broad categories of documentation: (1) background information to explain, underpin, support, and justify the establishment of the new program, and (2) the program document to describe the structure, curriculum, content, and regulations for the new program. The program document, when approved, is made available (through the library) to all students in the program to help guide them to undertake the program successfully. They suggest that the structured self-evaluation background information detail the following:

1. *Market demand and support:* documentary evidence on the need for the course in industry and society, of the potential student interest and of support from other internal and external stakeholders
2. *Accommodation/resources available to run program:* where the program is to be accommodated; specialized equipment and facilities required/available in school involved, kitchen/restaurant laboratory and lecture room accommodation, relevant library

stock, computer facilities, media resources; additional facilities and equipment required to run new program

3. *Staff:* identifying staff qualified to teach in the program, with their qualifications and detailed curricula vitae (CVs); the subjects to be taught by each, time allocations, including information on the rest of their duties; research, development, and general scholarship activities within the school involved, especially those which underpin the program and help to support its future development; staff professional development activities and plans

4. *Program management and quality assurance arrangements:* program management arrangements, membership of the program committee, individual year coordinators, tutoring arrangements; quality assurance and monitoring procedures, assessments, and examinations

5. *Program development plan:* detailed plans, giving duration, teaching and learning strategies, staff development, enhancement of facilities

6. *Any other documentation considered appropriate by the program planning team*

The main contents of the program document should comprise the following:

1. *Program background and structure:* introduction to the faculty, department, staff specialties, other programs currently offered, facilities available to run the programs, etc.; title of program, award sought, and date of submission, program aims and objectives; nature, duration, and general structure of program; relationships with professional and academic bodies, school and program advisory boards, etc.

2. *Admission criteria:* admission requirements and procedures, procedures for standard and non-standard applicants, advanced stage transfer procedures, etc.

3. *Curriculum, examinations, and syllabi:* program curriculum, class timetables giving contact hours, teaching methods (lecture, seminar, tutorials, workshops, practicals, others) and program credits; student workload; schedule of examinations, structure and weighting of each examination, marks and standards, regulations for progress to next stage, compulsory and optional program ele-

ments, compensation arrangements, diagrams showing alternative pathways through the program; details of each subject/component course, including aims (what lecturer wishes to achieve), objectives (what students will be able to do), general subject matter (including rationale and relevance to overall program and integration with other component courses), syllabus (detailed listing of contents of subject matter, with estimate of the learning hours required for each main section), strategy for delivery (teaching approach and methods), assessment and examination methods (including weightings), credits allocated (European Credit Transfer System, ECTS), and both essential and background reading lists (Duff et al., 2000a, pp. 66-67).

This documentation is then presented for comment and endorsement to the head of school, the heads of any collaborating schools, and as necessary to the heads of any external collaborating organizations. It is then forwarded to the Faculty Academic Board for consideration.

The Faculty Academic Board reviews the program documentation to assess its appropriateness for submission to a validation panel and to meeting the requirements of any external professional body involved. The Faculty Academic Board sets up a subgroup within the faculty to interact with the program planning team and to clarify the documentation. The program documentation approved by the Faculty Academic Board is forwarded to the Institute's Quality Assurance committee for validation.

VALIDATION AND ACCREDITATION

Validation is the formal process of assessing a proposed new program, and ensuring that it meets the requirements and standards for an academic award. The most favorable outcome of the validation process is the approval of the new program for delivery. In order to inform its judgment, the validation panel visits the school to consider the program documentation, discuss the proposed program with the planning team, lecturing staff, students, and graduates of the school, and to view the facilities available for the delivery of the program.

Composition of a Validation Panel

In order to enhance the rigor of the process, the Institute's quality assurance process prescribes that the validation panel includes both internal and external peers familiar with current practice and developments in the subject/discipline and who are independent of the school proposing the program. Members of the panel are usually chosen from those experienced in the practice of the discipline in industry, commerce, the public sector, or the profession. They possess some understanding of teaching, learning, assessment, and examination in undergraduate education. They are familiar with the institute or with similar institutes and have an awareness of the general requirements for the level of academic award proposed for the new program. The size of the validation panel is also a consideration because of the difficulty in assembling a large group of people with professional commitments for the number of days required for a validation event.

Typically, the validation panel includes:

- at least three persons from inside the institution including a chairperson, generally a senior academic from a faculty not involved in offering the program, a member with particular responsibility for quality assurance, and at least one member of staff not involved with the program, from the faculty proposing the program but from a school other than the one proposing the program; and
- at least two external members, nominated by the school and approved by the institute, one a senior academic in the discipline, and the other a senior professional or industrial practitioner in a related discipline. (DIT Quality Assurance Handbook, 1997)

A senior member of the quality assurance staff, independent of the school involved, should be nominated to act as secretary and organizer of the validation panel.

Role and Function of a Validation Panel

The validation panel is charged with making an impartial peer judgment on the standard, content, and implementation of the proposed program and on its comparability with similar programs elsewhere. It decides whether or not the graduates of the program should be eligible to be conferred with the proposed award.

The general issues considered and evaluated by the validation panel encompass the following:

1. *Program background and structure:* principles and philosophy underpinning the program (national and local relevance and demand) features; rationale for the development of the program; relationship of the program to the faculty/department plans and the institutional plans; aims and objectives; expected intellectual development and learning experience of a student taking the program

2. *Physical resources:* facilities required for the program and their suitability to ensure the standard proposed; lecture rooms, kitchen/restaurant laboratories, library, journals, IT access, other infrastructural support and their availability

3. *Staff:* staff profile, quality and level of staffing available to the program, availability to teach on it in the light of other commitments; research, scholarly, and professional work, publications, and staff development activities which underpin the standard of the program and help to ensure the maintenance of standards; recruitment and staff renewal policies and practices; liaison with other departments and faculties, with other undergraduate institutions in Ireland and abroad; liaison with industry, commerce, public agencies, professional bodies, and relevant international academic and other agencies

4. *Admission criteria:* clear student admission criteria at all stages, and criteria for student progression to the next stage of the program; projected student numbers, including mature students

5. *Curriculum, syllabi, and examinations:* program content appropriate to the aims and objectives determined; coherence; realizability of standards of the syllabi; how well the examination system proposed measures the extent to which students achieve the program objectives; appropriateness and progression of the syllabi throughout the program; integration of the different elements of the program; the academic standard in the award stage of the program

6. *Program management and quality assurance:* processes for managing the program through the program committee; tutors

and year coordinators; student support, counseling and tutoring arrangements, student handbook for the program, protection of students' rights; aspects of program which foster study skills, independent learning, individual responsibility, and professional behavior in students; international links and EU dimensions in the program; mechanisms for monitoring the program to maintain the standard of teaching, learning and student performance, including student feedback questionnaires and staff feedback schemes; mechanisms for innovation and improvement of the curriculum and reviewing the program at regular intervals; long-term program development plan and how it is proposed to put it into action. (DIT Quality Assurance Handbook, 1997; Duff et al., 2000a, p. 69)

Preparation for a Validation Event

The validation event includes a visit by the validation panel to the school proposing the new program. When the validation panel is appointed, each member should be supplied with a set of general briefing notes on the role and function of the validation panel, the program documentation prepared by the program planning team, the proposed timetable of the validation event, and any other relevant documentation. External members of the panel should be provided with background information about the institute. The circulation of the documentation should generally be completed in sufficient time for the panel members to study the documentation and to engage in any necessary consultations.

The chairperson of the program planning team undertakes the following duties in preparation for the validation event:

1. Ensuring that copies of the program documentation and all briefing documents are distributed to the members of the program planning team and other staff members involved with the program
2. Organizing meetings of the program planning team and other teaching staff who may be associated with the program, to discuss the documentation and to prepare to present the program and the program document to the validation panel

3. Inviting members of the program planning team and other teaching staff who may be associated with the program, as well as appropriate graduates and students to participate in the validation event

Validation Event

Activities may be scheduled for the validation event by the panel as follows:

1. Introduction of the panel to the senior staff of the faculty and school involved with the program, the chairperson of the program planning team, and other staff, as appropriate
2. Private meetings of the panel
3. Visit to facilities available to the program
4. Meetings with program planning team to discuss specific matters raised by the panel
5. Meeting with group of current students from comparable programs in the departments and faculties involved
6. Meeting with group of graduates from the departments and faculties involved
7. Meeting with staff members teaching in the program to discuss syllabi, teaching methods, examination, and such related issues (DIT Quality Assurance Handbook, 1997; Duff et al., 2000a)

The validation panel may divide into subgroups in order to facilitate its work, as it broadly seeks assurances on the following key questions:

1. Is there a clear need and demand for the program?
2. Are the aims and objectives of the program well-founded and clearly formulated?
3. Do the physical and human resources available and the curricula and teaching schemes proposed give realistic and achievable substance to these goals?
4. Do the examinations adequately test the students' learning on the program?

5. Do the graduates of the program possess knowledge, skills, and capabilities appropriate to the award? (DIT Quality Assurance Handbook, 1997; Duff et al., 2000a)

The panel chairperson seeks to clarify the aims of the validation event for the members of the panel, to guide discussion along the lines outlined above, and summarize the conclusions reached by the panel. The validation event should be conducted in a positive, constructive, and helpful manner leading to a productive outcome.

Report of the Validation Panel

At the end of the validation event, the chairperson may make an oral presentation of the findings and conclusions to the senior staff of the school and faculty. A written report indicating recommendation for approval or rejection of the proposed program is prepared by the validation panel who may also make suggestions for modifying the program and set special conditions or recommendations for approval.

The details contained in the report provide comments and recommendations on each of the following aspects of the validation process and for the proposed program:

- Program documentation provided
- Briefing documentation provided
- Schedule of the visit to the school
- Resources and facilities
- Staff
- Development of the program
- Findings with regard to the program and the award proposed
- Special conditions attached to the findings
- Other aspects of the program needing attention
- Any other relevant matters (DIT Quality Assurance Handbook, 1997)

Each member of the validation panel indicates approval by signing the report before it is forwarded to the Faculty Academic Board. A copy of the report is then circulated to the chairperson of the curriculum team for a formal response from the team, agreement by the head of the department, and then is forwarded with observations to the Faculty Academic Board. The report of the validation panel and the response of the course planning team are formally considered by the board and their observations are forwarded to the Institute Directorate.

Where the report from the validation panel sets conditions or makes recommendations requiring the proposed program to be modified, the planning program team carries out the additional work in response to the findings of the validation process. The revised program document is then returned for approval to the Faculty Academic Board. The Faculty Academic Board is charged with the responsibility for ensuring and confirming that the conditions and recommendations laid down by the validation panel have been satisfactorily addressed and appear in the revised program document. The revised program document, with confirmation that the stipulated conditions have been met, will be circulated for approval to all members of the validation panel.

When the program has received the final endorsement of the validation panel, and of the directorate, the faculty and school ensure that requisite details about the new program are included in the relevant prospectuses, public advertisements, and other publications for the information of prospective students.

Accreditation of a Program

Accreditation of a program is a process similar to validation, except that the authority giving approval to the program is usually an external organization, professional body, or academic institution. Normally, the procedure for accreditation is determined by the external organization and involves carrying out many or all of the stages of validation, described above, in cooperation with that organization.

Approved Program Document

The approved program document consists of a revised document, corrected and modified according to the agreed recommendations and conditions stipulated by the validation panel.

A copy of the approved program document is made available to the faculty director and a copy is placed in the faculty library before the program is scheduled to begin.

Student Handbook for the Program

A student handbook is prepared, by the program committee, for distribution to the students in the program. It is recommended to be as brief and clear as possible but should contain the following:

1. Welcome
    * Welcome by chairperson of the program committee
    * Introduction to the institution and a brief outline of its facilities
2. Program details
    * Duration of the program and minimum and maximum periods of registration
    * List of lecturers teaching in the program with brief details about their work and specialties
    * Class timetables
    * List of recommended textbooks and reference material
    * General schedule of examinations, relative weightings of subjects, arrangements for re-checks and appeals
    * Regulations for progression through the program
    * Recognition of the program by appropriate professional bodies
3. Program management
    * Program committee, program tutor, year coordinators/tutors, staff/student meetings, faculty authorities, examination boards, internal and external examiners, annual monitoring and review
    * Student feedback, staff/student meetings, student representatives on program committee, comments/suggestions box, student survey questionnaire
    * Program quality assurance procedures
4. Guidance to student
    * Attendance requirements
    * Calendar of academic year
    * Planning study program and study techniques

- Information on laboratory safety, production of reports
- Regulations for usage of computer facilities, library, other facilities
- General institution regulations on discipline, etc.
- Other relevant information, such as teaching locations, etc.
- Relevant student clubs (DIT Quality Assurance Handbook, 1997; Duff et al., 2000a, pp. 72-73)

SUMMARY

The process of curriculum quality assurance for a degree program in culinary arts identified in this chapter does not take full account of differing views, emphases, or emotional commitments to the particulars of the program or its subsets. These will be dealt with in a later chapter. However, it helps to focus the academic and professional orientation of the curriculum, based on the strengths of the curriculum team as well as the school and institute supporting the program.

Chapter 4

Guidelines for Quality Assurance in Curriculum Development for Culinary Arts Degree

Bringing the culinary arts degree program from an idea to validation requires that the quality assurance process must cover all phases of the curriculum development, including the environment and general context in which it is to be implemented. This chapter describes key factors in assuring culinary arts curriculum quality.

QUALITY ASSURANCE IN CURRICULUM IMPLEMENTATION AND MANAGEMENT

Normally, the head of the department and the program team serve as guarantors for the operation of the program. As early as possible in the initial intake, the program committee coopts student representative(s) into membership and engages, assembles, and selects a number of additional members onto the program committee as appropriate.

Staff Recruitment, Induction, and Development

The guiding principle for staff recruitment is that lecturers involved in teaching in an undergraduate degree program should possess qualifications at a level equivalent to, or, preferably, a level above the terminal award of the program and that subjects taught by lecturers should generally correspond to or be reasonably closely related to her or his core discipline(s) and qualification(s).

Teaching staff should be encultured in the educational philosophy, teaching practices, and facilities of the school. One suitable way of ensuring this is to engage in frequent mutual contact and communication by members of the school staff.

Role of the Program Committee in Operating a Program

The program committee, in close collaboration with the head of the department, is responsible for the operation of the program. It reports on the program to the faculty academic board. It prepares the student handbook for the program, organizes staff/student meetings, and deals with student, staff, and other feedback on the program and its operation. It processes nominations for internal and external examiners and monitors the range of examinations and examinations administered.

It prepares the annual review and monitoring report on the program. This report is often used to make decisions about the program's continuation, modification, expansion, or elimination in the context of limits of time, money, human energy, and capabilities which constrain schools from pursuing all possible good ends. It incorporates evaluation of progress made on the implementation of recommendations from previous annual reports, modifications to the program in the light of experience and new developments, staff, student, employer, and other feedback, and a thorough review of the strengths and weaknesses found in the program during the academic year. In the annual report, the program committee comments in particular on the incorporation of the suggestions of the external examiners, the outcome of the student examinations, retention and success rates, the need for staff development and other additional supports needed for the program. In best practice situations decisions in relation to the program's continuation, modification, expansion, or elimination are made in conjunction with the group responsible for the allocation of the institute's scarce resources.

The program committee assumes responsibility for critically reviewing the program every five years or so, and preparing the documentation for the review panel, as outlined later in this chapter.

Student Feedback

Student feedback on different aspects of a program needs to be obtained. The presence of student representatives from each year of a program on the program committee permits students' to bring to the attention of the program team points of view on whether the program achieves its objectives, as they arise. Meetings between members of the program committee and student representatives, general staff/student meetings, the use of student comments/suggestions boxes, can all be valuable ways of obtaining student feedback.

Another valuable and relatively open method for student feedback is the questionnaire, which can poll the views of the full student population in a program and allow those views to be graded and quantified. Such questionnaires should obtain graded feedback (very good, good, fair, poor) on the following issues with respect to each individual component or element of the program (lectures, seminars, tutorials, laboratory/restaurant work, field trips, industrial internship, project, etc.):

- Overall structure of the program
- Preparedness of student for the program
- Quality of the syllabus content and its relevance
- The balance between theory and practical work
- The relative time allocation to different program elements
- Appropriateness of assessment and examination methods
- Integration of the different program elements into the overall program
- Clarity and timeliness of information about the program
- The study/work time required on component programs
- Lecture/tutorial rooms
- Library facilities
- IT facilities and their accessibility
- Laboratories/restaurants/kitchens/studios
- Quality and quantity of equipment available
- Range of equipment available
- Standard of teaching and learning
- Punctuality of teachers
- Quality of tutorials
- Value of practical work
- Project management/supervision
- Method(s) of teaching
- Interactions with teacher/questions/discussion

- Responsiveness to student and other feedback
- Multimedia presentations and visual aids
- Classroom handouts
- Learning environment and ethos (DIT Quality Assurance Handbook, 1997; Duff et al., 2000a, p. 77)

Each individual lecturer is encouraged to administer a standard student survey questionnaire on each of her or his elements of the program. This allows her or him to analyze the responses and comments and adjust her or his teaching and presentation to correct perceived weaknesses. It also allows the lecturer to supply the program committee with a concise report of the responses and views of the students on her or his course, including any recommendations for improvement.

The program committee also administers a standard general student survey on the program as a whole, particularly to obtain the students' views on many of the issues listed above which are relevant to the program as a whole and its level of success in achieving the desired outcomes.

Feedback from Teaching Staff

Qualitative feedback should also be obtained by the program committee from the staff engaged in teaching in the program. A staff survey questionnaire is a simple method of obtaining this feedback which, as well as the matters listed above, should include the following:

- Preparedness of students for the program
- Student responsiveness and participation in the program
- Attendance and punctuality
- Integration of component parts of the program
- The administration of the program by the program committee
- Quality of communications with other lecturers
- Team teaching
- Responsiveness of the program course committee to suggestions
- Quality of leadership in the school and faculty
- Provision of resources
- Provisions for staff development (DIT Quality Assurance Handbook, 1997; Duff et al., 2000a, p. 78)

A key aspect of all procedures to obtain feedback on courses and programs is the need for the individual staff members, the program committee, the school and institutional management, as appropriate, to respond as well and as early as possible to it. The purpose of the feedback is to help to improve the program, to strengthen its weak links, and maintain its strong points. However, if the resources are not available to repair deficiencies, pointed out by students and/or staff, or appropriate measures are not taken to improve the program, this can contribute to student and staff demoralization and to degradation of the quality of the program and may result in its elimination.

ASSESSMENTS AND EXAMINATIONS

In any discussion on assessment there are at least three organizing questions to be addressed:

1. Why assess?
2. What to assess?
3. How to assess?

The first question is crucial, and how it is answered influences the school's approach to all aspects of assessment. Reasons for becoming involved in assessment were categorized by Leonard (1986) into areas of pedagogical, curricular, and political considerations.

What to Assess?

The answer to this question reflects the educational values in the school. Choices must be made on what to assess because it is not possible to assess everything. Options could entail simple and effective measurements that are subject specific and economical to administer or they might include a comprehensive approach which would entail monitoring students' progress throughout the program, giving equal attention to all aspects, and incorporating not only subject-specific learning, but cross-curricular and extracurricular learning. Such an approach also would assess personal and social attributes.

How to Assess?

A major drawback in the existing assessment and examination system in culinary arts is its narrow focus and summative nature. Law (1984) suggests that "traditional methods of assessment have shackled the curriculum by forcing teachers to pay attention to what they know is going to be assessed." By engaging in "a process of developing new criteria for assessment," Law predicts that the curriculum may be released from its shackles.

Examinations of various kinds—written, project, and practical examinations, oral and aural examinations, continuous assessments, examination of supervised professional practice and professional internship, examination of written reports and dissertations—are some of the methods which examiners use to measure the progress and performance of students in achieving the objectives of a program. Therefore they must become a core element in the assurance of academic quality in a program.

All examinations must be administered under clear procedures and formal written regulations. These need to be widely published and implemented transparently. Regulations may be general and cross-institution or course-specific as set out in the approved program document. In accepting a nomination as either internal or external examiner, a staff member or outside expert shall declare all relevant business, professional, or personal interests in respect of any candidates involved in the examinations concerned.

Internal Examiners

Internal examiners are normally full-time or part-time members of academic lecturing staff of the school. They are nominated by the relevant department head, and are appointed formally each year by the institution. Detailed duties and responsibilities of an internal examiner are set out in the regulations of the institution and made available to examiners. Each examiner must familiarize herself or himself with both the general and specific regulations in respect to the program(s) for which she or he is responsible. Broadly, internal examiners prepare and assess such examination materials as are required by the institution for the proper examination of the program(s) for which the examiners are responsible.

In relation to written examinations, internal examiners carry the following responsibilities:

- Submission of all draft examination papers in accordance with the dates and conditions specified by the institution
- Provision of marking schemes and outline answers or model solutions for each question on each examination paper
- Provision of clear instructions to students on each examination paper, specifying the number of questions to be attempted and the marks allocated for each question or part thereof
- Clear specification of when special materials or equipment are required or permitted at an invigilated examination and notification of these to the students in advance
- Ensuring the maintenance of the established standards for the program and conformity with examination specifications as set out in the regulations and the program document
- Employing consistency of terminology and clarity of expression in examination papers while maintaining the relevant standards and conventions of the discipline
- Ensuring that the content and overall balance of the examination paper is satisfactory, having regard to the syllabus and the standards of the course and the examination
- Where there is more than one internal examiner involved in the preparation of an examination paper, undertaking appropriate consultations concerning the formulation of the proper balance of the examination paper
- Giving due consideration to suggestions, criticisms, and amendments proposed by the external examiner(s)
- Ensuring that proof copies of examination papers are checked for accuracy
- Being available for consultation with the examinations office during the entire duration of the examination
- Collecting and signing for examination scripts from the examinations office and ensuring that the correct scripts in the correct quantity have been obtained
- When marking candidates' scripts, ensuring that marks awarded are in accordance with the marking scheme submitted and approved for the examination

- Marking scripts clearly, indicating the marks awarded to each examination question or part thereof attempted by the candidate
- In accordance with dates determined by the institution, returning all scripts and other assessed materials together with the marks sheet which shall clearly show the marks assigned to the various examination questions and the total mark expressed as a percentage
- Attending the examination board meeting for each program in which they are involved and participating in determining the overall examination result for each candidate
- Maintaining the strict confidentiality of the proceedings and deliberations of examination board meetings (DIT Quality Assurance Handbook, 1997; Duff et al., 2000a, pp. 79, 80)

In relation to coursework assignments that are subject to examination, the internal examiner has the following responsibilities:

- Notifying the students about the assignments prior to the commencement of the work, giving dates when such coursework should be submitted
- Ensuring that secure systems are in place for the handing in and receipt of coursework, and that information on the procedures to be followed by students in this regard is communicated to students
- Ensuring that appropriate criteria are established to assess the coursework and that examination procedures and standards correspond to best practice
- Giving students unambiguous information on the consequences of late submission of coursework

External Examiners

External examiners are most usually employed in respect of the program final year examinations, in order to provide an objective peer judgment on the standards achieved upon completion of the program. Each external examiner is normally appointed for a limited period, usually three years or the normal duration of the program. Occasionally, depending on the number of students and the number of specialties covered in the program, there may be more than one external examiner appointed.

Nominations for external examiners are made by the program committee and endorsed by the department head following informal consultation with the nominee to ascertain her or his willingness and availability to serve as an external examiner. Nominations are approved by the Academic Council in sufficient time to allow externs to have sight of, and approve draft examination papers and practical tests, at least six months in advance of the date of the first examination at which she or he is required to act.

An external examiner should normally hold academic or professional qualifications similar to or higher than the award from the program to be examined. She or he should be of some eminence in the relevant academic field and/or the professional practice of the discipline. The head of the department is normally the sole contact person between the institution and the external examiner in relation to examination matters.

When the appointment of an external examiner is confirmed, the institute formally notifies her or him, providing details of the appointment together with a range of briefing documents including the approved program document, previous examination papers, and schedules for the forthcoming examinations and examination boards. These briefing documents should also contain information about the duties of external examiners in relation to draft examination papers, examination scripts, project reports, oral examinations and examination boards, and any other relevant information. This liaison with the external examiner is carried out at the earliest possible stage by the head of the department, to enable the external examiner to carry out the duties involved.

The external examiner reviews draft examination papers, including sample model marking schemes, and provides comments on these to the department head. After the examination scripts have been marked, the external examiner visits the school. She or he examines a representative sample of the candidates' marked examination scripts and/or other examination materials such as candidates' assessed coursework, and may interview candidates as deemed appropriate. The external examiners are not employed for the purpose of directly examining/marking the work of candidates, but rather to monitor the examination process. The internal and external examiners, in consultation with the head of the department, normally agree on the marks to be presented to the examination board. The external examiner attends the examination board meeting in which the overall results for the candidates are decided. The ultimate function of the external examiner is to ensure that the results achieved by each candidate in the overall examination are comparable to similar programs both nationally and internationally. Each year, at the end of the examination process, the external examiner presents a written report on the general standards reached by the candidates, giving comments on the overall conduct of the program and examinations, and making suggestions for any improvements.

Conduct of Examinations

The conduct of written and practical examinations requires special attention. Before candidates are admitted to the examination, the room must be set out with the materials required for the particular examination(s) to be held, and a clock must be clearly visible to each candidate. Only candidates in possession of examination admission documentation should be permitted into the examination hall and each should sign the attendance form and sit in her or his designated place. No unauthorized materials such as computing equipment, electronic organizers, programmable calculators, mobile phones, pagers, radios, tape-recorders, books, notes, papers, drawings, or other materials may be brought into the examination room.

The examination invigilator supplies any authorized materials to the candidates—examination papers, answer books, tables, etc.—and ensures that candidates are in possession of the correct examination papers before announcing the start of the examination. During the examination, candidates must be supervised constantly to ensure that they do not engage in unfair practices or activities likely to cause disturbance to other candidates. In the event of a query from any candidate concerning an examination paper the invigilator refers this to the examinations office for resolution by the internal examiner. Any clarification or correction provided is brought to the attention of all relevant candidates. The invigilator records such matters in a report that is subsequently made available to the examination board.

Also, the invigilator implements the rules relative to candidates who leave the examination room during any period of the examination either without or with permission. In either case, the invigilator records the event and the candidate's examination number. In the case where a candidate leaves without permission, such a candidate will not be readmitted during that examination. Where a candidate is given permission to leave the examination room for personal needs, or because of becoming distressed or ill, she or he must be accompanied at all times by an invigilator. In the event of a candidate continuing with the examination, a time extension equal to the period of absence from the examination room may be granted, at the discretion of the examinations secretary.

Normally, no candidate can be admitted to the examination hall more than one half hour after the start of the examination. In exceptional circumstances, and provided that no other candidate taking the same exam has withdrawn and left the examination room, a candidate may be admitted later, at the discretion of the examinations secretary. In such circumstances extra time is not normally allowed.

The invigilator announces the end of the examination period, ensures that candidates stop writing when instructed to do so, and submit all answer books and other materials for examination. The invigilator ensures that candidates remain seated while the scripts and other materials are being collected. She or he records the number of scripts submitted by each candidate and completes the invigilator's report. All of the candidates' scripts, all surplus unused answer books, examination question papers, and other materials, together with the attendance sheet and the invigilator's report, are then returned to the examinations office.

Marking of Examinations

The internal examiner is required to mark—anonymously—each candidate's script clearly, ensuring that the marks awarded accord with those set out in the approved marking scheme, and that all attempted questions are marked. She or he must also ensure that the marks awarded are transferred accurately to summary sheets, in preparation for the examination board. These are two stages in which errors can easily arise and it is highly advisable that a team of colleagues be nominated within the school to check and recheck that the scripts are fully marked and that the marks have been correctly transferred.

The examination of satisfactory completion of coursework undertaken—practical kitchen and restaurant laboratory work, essays, projects, and other assignments—presents certain challenges. Assignments to be examined, the submission dates, including penalties for late submission, must be notified clearly to students in ample time. The actual submission also needs to be carefully recorded as well as any backup procedures. The internal examiner is required to establish appropriate examination criteria and procedures for coursework, which correspond to the best practice in the relevant discipline.

Breaches in examination rules, abuses and unfair practices by candidates in written examinations and assigned work, such as plagiarism and copying other persons' work, need to be specified carefully, together with the resulting penalties.

Examination Boards

Examination boards determine the results for the overall examination process in a given year of a program prior to the candidate being allowed to proceed to the next year or be awarded the final award of the program. The membership of the examination board includes

- all internal and external examiners duly appointed for the program,
- all heads of the departments involved with the program,
- the head of faculty or her or his representative, usually acting as chairperson,
- any approved representative of an external body, as observer, and
- a representative of the examinations office, as observer (DIT Quality Assurance Handbook, 1997; Duff et al., 2000a, p. 84).

Only members of the examination board may attend its meeting(s). All members undertake to maintain strict confidentiality with regard to the deliberations of the examination board in relation to - individual candidates, with the examination process in general, and individual examiners. Department heads may only discuss details of the examination results with the candidates concerned and members of the examination board but not with third parties.

The examination board is guided by the general institute's examination regulations, the specific regulations for the program as specified in the approved program document and the principles of natural justice. Any special circumstances that might have an influence on a candidate's performance and have been notified in writing to the institute authorities must be brought to the attention of the examination board. The board generally aims to reach its decisions by consensus, but if this is not possible, a majority vote, including one in which the chairperson may exercise a casting vote, determines the decision in any case.

Candidates are notified in the clearest possible way of the results of the deliberations of the examination board, including the overall result, the marks for individual subject elements, and any requirements for reexamination. This must be provided in writing for each candidate as soon as possible after the examination board meets.

Consideration of Examination Results

Examination results are one of the measures of the success of a program and its delivery and are therefore a key component of quality assurance. It is vital that the responsible department heads and the program committee systematically consider the results to extract the main lessons and use them to plan program improvements.

The department head, in consultation with the program committee, is responsible for preparing a summary report on the examination results, to give the following details in respect of each stage/year of the program, and in respect of females and males:

- Number of students registered
- Number of candidates enrolled for the examination
- Number who presented
- Overall number who passed
- Numbers who achieved each honors grade
- Number who achieved a pass grade
- Number who gained exemptions and related credits
- Number ineligible to continue

- Subjects and subject elements with average marks above overall average, with comments and explanations
- Subjects and subject elements with average marks below overall average with comments and explanations
- Comments on results and comparison with previous years stages and with comparable programs in the faculty (DIT Quality Assurance Handbook, 1997; Duff et al., 2000a, p. 85)

External Examiner's Report to the School

The external examiner makes a formal written report to the school on the overall examination process, as soon as possible after the examination board meeting. This report should contain comments and suggestions on each of the following areas:

- Presentation and timeliness of the draft examination papers
- Structure, organization, balance, and standard of the examination papers
- Marking of the examination papers, projects, and other written presentations
- Overall performance of the candidates, particularly in comparison with their peers nationally and internationally
- Academic standard achieved by the candidates
- Weaknesses evident in the examinations/program
- Recommendations to improve the organization and administration of the examination system
- Other suggestions and recommendations for the program committee
- Suggestions and recommendations to the institution
- Any other comments (DIT Quality Assurance Handbook, 1997; Duff et al., 2000a, p. 85)

The external examiner's report is a key element in the assurance of academic quality and in the evaluation of the program. It is returned to the department head, who considers any issues of immediate concern needing to be resolved by the school or institute authorities and circulates copies to the chairperson of the program committee for appropriate action. The recommendations should be discussed by the program committee and included in the annual monitoring report on the program.

The key points and recommendations of the external examiner's report are also attached to the report by the department head on the overall examination results for the program, which, together with comments by the faculty academic board, is forwarded to the institute's Academic Council.

DISCIPLINARY PROCEDURES

A candidate who breaches the examination regulations through cheating, plagiarism, misrepresentation, bribery, falsification, impersonation, and other forms of deception, including the possession of examination papers in advance of the examination, is subject to disciplinary procedures. A breach of regulations constituting unfair practice may be detected during the examination of any coursework for which credit is obtained, during invigilated examinations, or during the marking of written examination scripts.

In each case, the examiner and/or invigilator documents and reports the incident immediately to the department head, including all relevant material(s) confiscated. The head of the department then initiates the formal inquiry procedures of the institution. An inquiry into an allegation of a breach of the examination regulations are conducted by a duly constituted panel of inquiry.

The head of the department presents a written report to the panel of inquiry and attends a hearing of the panel to respond to the matters raised. A copy of this report is provided to the candidate prior to the first hearing of the panel. The head of the department should be present at the panel of inquiry for as long as the candidate and her or his representative are present.

The candidate is notified in writing through the office of the faculty administrator at least a week in advance of the meeting of the panel of inquiry in relation to the precise allegation(s), her or his entitlement to present a response either orally or in writing to the panel and be accompanied at all hearings conducted by the panel, and the inquiry schedule. The candidate notifies the faculty administrator of the person(s) to accompany them, and their status at a meeting of the panel of inquiry.

The panel of inquiry assembles to consider the allegation(s) as soon as possible following the reporting of the incident. Each case is considered separately and only on the basis of unambiguous evidence presented. The head of the department and the candidate are entitled to call witnesses and notice of their intention in this regard must be provided to the parties involved at least one working day prior to the date on which the witnesses are scheduled to attend. The candidate must have the right to cross-examine witnesses.

The panel of inquiry alone adjudicates on the allegations(s) based on the written and oral submissions and determines the penalty to be applied. Other than an administrative secretary, no other person shall be present during the period of adjudication. The candidate is notified in writing, through the office of the faculty, of the outcome of the inquiry. The decision of the panel of inquiry is final.

In circumstances where the outcome of the panel of inquiry may require an alteration of an examination board decision, then the board reconvenes to consider that decision. The examination board should have no function or authority in determining the facts of a case of an allegation of a breach of the examination regulations.

Where a breach of the examination regulations involving a significant number of the candidates is suspected, then the institute may refer the matter to the panel of inquiry. A decision in relation to the status of the examination involved and whether or not that examination shall be rescheduled shall be the responsibility of the panel of inquiry. In such circumstances, all of the candidates who might be affected by such a decision shall have the right to make submissions to the panel of inquiry before a decision is made. The panel of inquiry also has the power to declare the examination to be void in respect to some candidates only.

Where the panel of inquiry deems the candidate guilty of a breach of the regulations, it determines the actual penalty to be applied along the following lines, having regard to the seriousness of the incident.

- It may issue a written warning to the candidate, which constitutes a formal record of breach of regulations.
- It may deem the candidate to have failed all or part of the examinations for the stage or year of the program, and determines the

period of time that shall elapse before the candidate is entitled to be reassessed.

- It may determine that the candidate is ineligible for any special award of the institution.
- It may suspend the candidate from all activities of the institution for a stated period.
- It may recommend to academic council the expulsion of the candidate from the institution.

STUDENT APPEALS

Clear and well-publicized procedures for candidates to appeal the decision of an examination board must be accessible to all students. These procedures must expedite the resolution of an appeal, as early as possible and at as close proximity to the student as possible. Thus a candidate considering an appeal should discuss the issue(s) with the head of the department. In response, the head of the department should carry out a recheck of the examination script(s), establishing that all attempted parts of each question were marked, and that no error occurred during the marking process or in the transfer of marks to the result sheet.

This process may give rise to the need for a review of the examination script, to establish that all answers, part answers, and/or other examination materials have been correctly assessed in accordance with the model marking scheme and have been correctly determined. Normally two internal examiners, different from those directly involved, are nominated by the head of the department to perform the review. In the event of the outcome of a review giving rise to a significant change of grade, it shall be open to the head of the department to require a complete review of all examination scripts in the subject concerned.

Should either of these processes change the result for the candidate, the examination board must be reconvened to formally change the result. If the outcome of these processes is not acceptable to the candidate, and a valid basis for an appeal exists, she or he may seek to make her or his case to the appeals board. The valid bases for an appeal are normally one or more of the following grounds, where it is claimed that

- the examination regulations of the institution, either general or specific to the program, were not properly implemented;
- circumstances existed which may not have been covered by the examination regulations; or
- compassionate circumstances exist which relate to a candidate's examination situation (not to the period of the program before that).

The appeals board is formally constituted by the academic council and can function only with an agreed quorum. Decisions of the appeals board are normally formulated by consensus but where this is not feasible the outcome is determined by a majority decision. The appeals board is not empowered to make any change retrospectively to the examination regulations for the examination involved in the appeal.

An appeal must be lodged in the faculty office on a standard form normally within one week of the outcome of the school process. Late appeals may be considered only in exceptional circumstances. Appeals must be heard by the appeals board as soon as possible after its submission. An appellant must have the right to present her or his case personally to the appeals board and/or to be represented by a third party. The decision of the appeals board is final and binding on both the institute and the appellant.

ANNUAL MONITORING REPORT

In order to assure the academic quality of each program, and to enable the course committee reviewing the implementation of the curriculum to continuously improve it, an annual monitoring report on the functioning of the program in the previous academic year is prepared by the program committee and submitted through the head of the school/department to the faculty academic board during the first term of each academic year.

The purpose of the annual monitoring report (Form Q5) is to critically evaluate the program and its implementation, to ensure academic standards are maintained, and that an active program of development and improvement for the program is put in place. It allows the program committee to review the relevance of the program in light of external developments in technology and in society. It provides an opportunity to assess the effectiveness of the continuous monitoring of the program throughout the academic year, and to record and implement corrective measures and other modifications for program improvement. The main elements of the annual monitoring report on the program are the examination results, prepared in respect of each year of the program, and the program monitoring/quality ratings (DIT Quality Assurance Handbook, 1995, 1997).

Examination Results

In addition, an extract of the key points of the external examiner's report together with a copy of the report by the head of the department on the overall examination results for the program, with comments by the faculty director, constitutes the first part of the annual monitoring report.

Program Monitoring Report/Quality Rating

The program committee carries out the other part of the annual program monitoring/quality rating for the program by accumulating the following data, observations, and recommendations about the program:

- A summary of the recommendations of the previous annual report (or five-yearly review) and the subsequent actions on the key recommendations, as inserted in the approved program document
- Performance indicators for the year, giving target and actual student numbers enrolled, student/staff ratio figures, significant developments and factors affecting the program during the academic year, summary highlights of examination statistics, pass/fail/retention/other numbers, details of the placement of graduates and a summary of feedback from the students and staff
- Key comments from external examiners' reports
- An overview of the key issues affecting the program delivery, especially those needing remedial attention, and the development plan for the coming academic year including an examination of the program delivery, weaknesses and remedial measures to be

taken, measures to be taken arising from the student feedback and from recommendations of the external examiners, measures to be taken on resource issues and on related academic developments including recruitment, staff professional development, research, and scholarship

- Proposed modifications to the program, especially those involving changes in examination regulations, must be recorded accurately and included in the annual updating of or amendments to the approved program document.
- Quality ratings for key aspects of the course including staffing, accommodation, equipment, teaching standards, learning environment, and job placement of graduates (The range of ratings might include *very good, good, fair,* and *poor.*)
- Comments by the chairperson of the program committee about the effectiveness of the functioning of the program committee
- Comments by the head of the department on the report, the quality ratings assigned by the program committee, and issues relating to the program development plan
- Overall quality rating by the faculty board, on the scale from very good to poor, and comments by the faculty head (DIT Quality Assurance Handbook, 1997; Duff et al., 2000a, pp. 85-86)

Indicative Guidelines for Quality Ratings

The following are general guidelines to allocating quality ratings on the four-point scale: *very good, good, fair,* and *poor.* The use of such ratings allows the year-to-year changes, improvements and disimprovements, to be charted and highlighted.

Very good. The program has well-founded objectives and a well organized and directed teaching program. The staff members are well qualified and highly motivated, some are engaged in relevant research and/or industrial collaboration, and they have good quality office accommodations and facilities. The lecture rooms, laboratories, and other student accommodations are of a high quality, well designed and with a range of appropriate projection, video, and computer-based display methods available. Equipment and other resources are of an advanced standard and accessible to the students in the program. Classes in the program are characterized by good teaching at a demanding level and challenging and relevant student assignments. Students are deeply and intelligently involved, show evidence of thorough learning, including considerable self-learning, and appropriate progression, and are provided with regular feedback on their progress and with advice and guidance based on their examinations and other work. The oral and written work of the students is generally of a high standard. Graduates of the program obtain immediate employment or embark on further studies.

Good. The program has many, but not all, of the features above but possibly some negative features. There may be more part-time teachers involved than is desirable, some staff may not be as up-to-date as desirable, and their facilities may be limited. The teaching accommodations may have some limitations with lecture rooms that may be overcrowded, and requisite resources may not always be adequate. There may be equipment shortages in some areas or some equipment may not be quite up-to-date. Teaching is above average but possibly not sharply focused or integrated. Student response may be good but could be improved, there may be little self-learning occurring, and there may be some weakness in students' oral and/or written work. Overall, the program quality is healthy and gives students ample opportunities to progress in most areas of the program, but improvements may be slow. Some graduates of the program may feel that it has not equipped them fully to obtain some employment or may feel unprepared for further studies.

Fair. The program is at an adequate mainstream level of quality, with some weaknesses counterbalanced by strengths. Staff may be complacent and continue to present the program in a routine manner from one year to the next. Accommodations may be broadly acceptable but with some limitations on amount and/or standard. There may be little advanced equipment available for student use. Teaching may not be student-centered and may concern mainly factual information, with content reliable and solid but uninspiring. The response and work of the students is adequate but mixed and only a few students reach what might be estimated as their full potential. The learning environment may be characterized by lack of excitement and challenge. Graduates have some trouble gaining employment. The program urgently requires a fundamental self-study and review.

Poor. The program has some critical weaknesses in conception, integration, delivery, or resources. Many staff members may be complacent and are not striving to inspire. The accommodations and facilities available are deficient in a number of areas and teaching resources may be rather basic or primitive. Some teaching may be poorly conceived and organized, and ill-matched to the capabilities of some of the students. Objectives are vague or are not met. The pace is slow and there may be little encouragement or possibility of independent student learning. Standards achieved in student oral and written work are sometimes not adequate for the level of award. The learning environment tends to be routine and moribund. Graduates have difficulty in finding employment directly and often feel they must work for additional qualifications. The program should be terminated or overhauled completely (DIT Quality Assurance Handbook, 1997; Duff et al., 2000a, pp. 88-89).

CONSIDERATION OF THE ANNUAL MONITORING REPORT

The annual monitoring report is first considered within the school and approved by the head of the department and the measures and improvements recommended in the report should be approved and decided at this level to the extent possible within the resources and budget of the school. The report is then forwarded to the faculty academic board where the proposed actions to ensure enhanced academic content and its delivery are reviewed. Where some additional resources are required, these are considered by the faculty executive whose responsibility it is to make such additional resources available. The annual monitoring report, together with details of the specific measures taken and comments by the head of the department and the faculty director is forwarded to Academic Council. The approved annual monitoring report on the program is forwarded by the department head to each external examiner for her or his information. In the case of externally accredited programs, the annual monitoring report may also be forwarded to the external accrediting organization.

Each year the Academic Council, generally through a Quality Assurance subcommittee, considers in detail the program annual monitoring reports from across the institute. Following this consideration, this Quality Assurance subcommittee may meet representatives from the program committee or require the program committee or the faculty academic board to give special attention to particular issues raised during the annual monitoring process.

Modifications to a Program Before the Five-Year Review

As a result of the annual monitoring report, modifications to the program may be proposed. If the faculty academic board or Academic Council considers that any proposed program modifications are substantial, they may decide that a full or partial program review is necessary and request the faculty director to initiate such a process.

All modifications made to a program curriculum or examination regulations of any component subject or subject element, as a result of the annual monitoring report, must be documented. Copies of all such amendments should be forwarded to the department head, faculty director, faculty library, and Academic Council, in advance of the next academic session. The amended program document then becomes the current approved program document.

Periodic Critical Self-Evaluation and Review

Each program conducted within an institute should be subject to periodic review, normally on a five-year cycle or more frequently as required by academic council, faculty academic board, or program committee. These five-year reviews are an opportunity for the program committee and program team to reappraise the program and to make major modifications to it, if considered appropriate.

Where major modifications to a program are being proposed, the program committee should consult the faculty academic board to obtain approval for such modifications. In some cases, where extensive modifications with serious resource implications and/or implications for other programs in the faculty are envisioned, it may be necessary for the faculty board to obtain full program planning approval from the institute's authorities.

Critical Self-Study by the Program Committee

The main process involved in the review of a program is the fundamental, critically reflexive self-study or self-analysis and reappraisal of all aspects of the curriculum by the program committee. This reflexive self-study is designed to assist the program committee to improve the program. Therefore, it should be a comprehensive review, derived at least partly from the annual monitoring reports/quality ratings of the program for the period since the initial validation or the previous periodic review, and also from a clear understanding of developments in the culinary arts discipline, in food services industry, and in society. It is an evaluation of the effectiveness of various aspects of the program, giving due recognition to problem areas as well as good features and achievements. The reflexive self-study results in a thorough and concise report that aims to be a critically constructive statement of the views of the program committee on the overall quality of the teaching and learning in the program, and how it is to be developed.

The following aspects of the program should be reflected upon in the critical self-study report:

- Aims and objectives of the program and its continuing relevance to the aims of the department, faculty, and institution; relevant industrial, commercial, and professional developments; impact of government and EU policies and regulations; job placement of graduates; feedback from employers
- Admission requirements and standards of those admitted, intake policy and procedures, transfers into the program at advanced stages, mature students, numbers progressing through the program
- Program structure and content, student workload, subject delivery, optional subjects and elements, teaching techniques
- Accommodations for the program, teaching facilities and resources, library, IT, and other learning resources
- Technical and administrative support
- Student placement for work experience, international student exchanges.
- Examinations, examination results, external examiners' reports, arrangements for annual monitoring, quality ratings
- Membership of program committee, operation of program committee, year coordinators/tutors, program advisory board, student handbook, and other information channels to students, feedback from students, relevant student societies

- Staff members teaching in the program, their qualifications, involvement in research and scholarly activities and achievements, staff professional development, international staff exchanges, research underpinning the program, professional and industrial involvement
- Outcomes of the previous program development/review plans

Details of major enhancements to the program, arising from the reflective self-study should be clearly indicated with the rationale for introducing them. In the same context, a medium-term program development plan should also be elaborated, comprising the following aspects:

- Detailed plans for the future development of program, giving time-scale
- Staff professional development plans
- Teaching and learning enhancement plans
- Plans for improved annual monitoring of the program

The reflective self-study report is prepared by the program committee in consultation with the program team, the staff members involved in teaching the program who are generally most aware of the strengths and weaknesses of the program. In preparing the reflective self-study, the program committee consults with the major stakeholders, namely, students and graduates of the program, and industry and business people, government, and other external organizations, as appropriate. The self-study process therefore presents an ideal opportunity for those delivering the program to enhance its quality and interaction, and indeed to impress their general ownership and identity upon it. The self-study also enables the review panel to highlight key areas for attention and facilitates the subsequent work of the faculty academic board in monitoring the implementation of the recommendations of the review panel.

Documentation Required for Review Event

The documentation required for a review event includes a written critically reflective self-study and the program document, as described earlier in relation to the validation process (see Chapter 3).

This program document should incorporate the considerations and recommendations arising during the self-study process. The program committee may supply any other documentation deemed useful for the review event.

These documents are submitted for endorsement to the head of the department involved and the head of any external collaborating organization. They are then forwarded to the faculty academic board which reviews the program documentation in a manner similar to its consideration of the documentation submitted for a validation event. When the program documentation is approved, the Academic Council is advised and a request for a review panel and a review event is made.

PROGRAM REVIEW

The main external peer-review section of the review is carried out by a review panel which is required to make an impartial judgment on the continued achievement of the overall standard of the program and on its acceptability for the award, when compared with similar programs nationally and/or internationally.

Academic Council, in consultation with the faculty academic board, is responsible for constituting the review panel, which is typically similar in composition to a validation panel as described in Chapter 3. A candidate for membership of a review panel who has served as an external examiner in the program should have completed her or his external examinership at least two years prior to the review event.

In order to complete its work, the review panel visits the school to review the program documentation, discuss the program with the program committee, students, and graduates of the program, and view the facilities available for conducting the program. The review event typically has a timetable similar to a validation event. The general issues considered and evaluated by a review panel encompass all of the issues considered by a validation panel but with an emphasis on the following aspects of the internal review:

- Quality and comprehensiveness of the self-study of the program
- Principles and philosophy underpinning the self-study and their relevance to the program

- Evidence of program improvements in annual monitoring/quality rating reports
- Logic of the detailed recommendations arising from the self-study
- Appropriateness of the proposed changes to the program to fulfill these recommendations
- Overall health of the program and procedures for academic quality assurance within it

The review panel focuses mainly on the critical self-study report prepared by the program committee and examines the revised program document, mainly to ensure that there is correlation between the conclusions of the self-study and the program document and that any significant changes proposed are both appropriate and recorded.

At the end of the review visit, the chairperson of the review panel may provide an oral presentation of the findings and conclusions of the panel to the faculty director, head of the department, and chairperson of the program committee. This presentation may indicate a recommendation for continuing approval of the program, or make suggestions for modifying the program or outline special conditions for continuing approval. The review panel prepares a written report, following the format of the program validation report. The confirmed and endorsed report is forwarded to the head of the department. Consideration of the review panel report at the program committee, school, and faculty academic board levels follows the same pattern described in Chapter 3 for a validation panel report.

TERMINATION OF A PROGRAM

An approved program may be discontinued only with the approval of Academic Council on the recommendation of the faculty academic board and the executive authorities of the institute. Where an approved program does not operate for two years due to lack of student demand or lack of resources, its period of approval should lapse unless the reasons for the non-operation of the program have had prior acceptance from the faculty authorities. If the program approval lapses in this way, the head of the department will be required to resubmit the program for validation and approval before it is offered again (DIT Quality Assurance Handbook, 1995, 1997).

Chapter 5

The Role of Reflexivity in Assuring Curriculum Quality in Culinary Arts

Reflexivity is a methodological tool that has a great deal to offer culinary arts educators, practitioners, and researchers. It allows practitioners to think critically about their practices. It allows educators to become critically reflexive in their practice as teachers. It facilitates culinary arts researchers and allows them to become resource persons, offering guidelines and suggesting approaches to critical thinking and problem-solving. Reflexivity engages culinary arts educational researchers in exploring the learning/teaching process in a manner that enhances the development of culinary arts knowledge. It involves both the study of a situation with a view to improving the quality of the action within it and in challenging the traditional orthodoxy of culinary arts education with a view to improving it. That is, challenging the structure and sequence of the traditional professional cookery program with teachers telling students what to do, students working with little idea of the final outcome, and teachers punishing the whole class for one student's inability or unwillingness to carry out the teacher's instructions uncritically. In the reflexive context, these are seen as learning problems in which the realization of practice, time, and patience provide a framework for resolving both the teacher's and the students' problem by increasing the consciousness that the teacher and the student both need time to learn. Effective teaching is having the patience to wait for the signal that new skills have been learned.

Text on pages 86-87 has been quoted from *Millennium: Journal of International Studies.* This article first appeared in *Millennium,* Volume 20, No. 3, 1991, and is reproduced with the permission of the publisher.

However, a word of caution is necessary. Reflexivity calls for a paradoxical stance toward the questions of "certainty" and "objectivity." The dilemma faced by the beginning reflexive researcher or teacher is the realization that there is no "given," "pre-objectified" state of affairs waiting to be uncovered through inquiry. The "truth" is that most research findings, whether achieved through reflexive or other modes, are someone's construction of "reality." The role of the educational researcher is to test the construction of the situation by bringing to the surface and discriminating among alternative presentations that may offer different perspectives on reality.

REFLECTION, REFLEXIVITY, REFLECTIVE THINKING: A NEVER-ENDING DANCE

Reflective accounts of educational research are relatively recent and are to be found in a limited range of publications (Bassey, 1999, p. 6). In the reflection/reflexivity in education research literature many collections of individual stories are encountered and are used to facilitate reflection and to record a reflective response to some immediate situation (Burgess, 1984; Schon, 1987, 1991; Steier, 1991). Reflective storytelling as a research method is less a matter of the application of a positive/scholarly technique to understanding phenomena than it is a matter of entering into the phenomena, participating in it, and reflecting on and giving meaning to the experience. Reflection is not, by definition, critical. It is quite possible to engage in curriculum development while focusing on the nuts and bolts of the process. Just because reflection is not critical does not mean that it is unimportant or unnecessary. Reflection becomes critical when it has distinctive purposes leading to uncovering paradigmatic, structuring assumptions such as, in this case, merging liberal and vocational education in an integrated manner and creating a new curriculum model for advanced study in culinary arts. There are human considerations of positional and expert power or lack of it and how it undergirds, frames, or distorts educational processes and interactions. Reflection becomes critical when it questions assumptions and practices in our professional lives. Reflection is a matter of stance and dance. My stance toward my analysis is one of engaging in constant reflective inquiry, always needing further investigation, reflection, and renewal. My dance is the dance of experimentation and risk, working at the edge of what was possible in terms of the giant step for a culinary arts school to take. Critical reflection is a hopeful activity. It is engaged in a spirit full of hope for the future. In the current context, reflexivity is the engagement of culinary arts researchers, educators, and practitioners seeking to understand the meaning of the world of culinary arts as higher education, and avoiding the traps of a structure constructed without an understanding of the meanings. The hope is that the reflective process will bring to culinary arts curriculum development an awareness of taken-for-granted assumptions and tacit theories, and so enable articulation and transformation to occur in the manner of the work, in order to improve it.

Reflective research, according to Alvesson and Skoldberg (2000, p. 5), has two basic characteristics: careful interpretation and reflection. The first implies that all references—trivial and nontrivial—to empirical data are the results of interpretation that comes to the forefront of the research work. This calls for an awareness of theoretical assumptions, the importance of language and pre-understanding, all of which constitute major determinants of the interpretation. The second element, reflection, turns attention "inward" toward the person of the researcher, the relevant community of scholars, practitioners, and society as a whole, the intellectual and cultural traditions and the central importance, as well as the problematic nature of language and narrative in the research context. Reflection can be identified as the interpretation of interpretation and the launching of critical self-exploration of one's own interpretation of empirical material, including its construction.

ADVANTAGE OF REFLECTIVE ETHNOGRAPHY IN CULINARY ARTS CURRICULUM DEVELOPMENT

Reflective ethnography in culinary arts curriculum development employs participant observation and reflection upon it as the dominant research strategy. In the 1970s, several research societies were formed around the aim of stimulating and coordinating the ethnographical, anthropological, and historical study of food habits. During the 1970s and 1980s, the topic of food gained in popularity and a process of diversification and specialization has been under way ever since. In the mid-1990s, the first discussions on EthnoCulinary Arts took place (Hegarty, 1996). This development resulted in, among other things, reflection, generalization, and theory development. By such methods, one enters the world of the persons or groups being studied in an attempt to hear and understand their shared meanings and taken for granted assumptions. Ethnography not only implies engagement of the researcher in the world under study; it also implies a commitment to search for meaning, a suspension of preconceptions, and an orientation toward discovery. In other words, ethnography involves risks, uncertainty, and discomfort. Reflective ethnography was chosen as a methodology to engage with curriculum development in culinary arts not because of an intrinsic belief in the superiority of one method of educational research to develop understanding, but because of a belief that the methodology was suitable in meeting the criteria suggested by Silverman (1997, p. 25), namely, that the researcher has demonstrated successfully why she or he should be believed and that the research problem tackled has any theoretical/practical significance.

The culinary arts department head is advised to read as many reflective ethnography accounts of curriculum and school development as possible in order to develop a deep understanding of the process. The ascribed value of such an exercise is that the stories "give practitioners reason" (Schon, 1991, pp. 5-9). It questions the activities of those engaged in curriculum and school development and encourages them to question themselves in the context of their own practices over a protracted period of time. Also, it involves observing and participating in the curriculum and school development process, and reflecting on what is going on, and in what is really going on under the guise of these developments. School and curriculum development happens, but something else happens also, namely self-reflection—a search for "self," for "voice," and "authorship." Researchers describe what they observe and try to illuminate what practitioners actually say and do, by exploring understandings revealed through the process of the spontaneous activity that makes up their practice. Whenever the patterns appear strange or paradoxical to the authors, in their role as researchers, they seek to discover the underlying sense. They are forced sometimes to reflect on their own understandings and interpretations of their subjects' understandings; and sometimes cause the reader also to engage in reflection on the understanding and interpretation of both the researcher and the subject. By means of this reflection on reflection (reflexivity) the sense in someone else's ethnography emerges. Also, practitioners reflect on and question their own performance. The reflective ethnography school accepts that the researcher affects the research while engaging in it. The reflective ethnography school seeks to establish and to legitimize experience as a valid and reliable research method. Doing reflective ethnography can be seen to mirror the way we go about thinking and researching issues in everyday life. The only way to learn about reflective ethnography is to do it. The only way to do it better is to do more of it. Reflective ethnography relies on the engagement of the self. It is this kind of self-conscious engagement that defines the process and rigor of the methodology. The basis of the rigor is the conscious and deliberate linking of the process of self-engagement in the field with the technical processes of data collection, analysis, and decisions that such linking involves. This linking or bending back is reflexivity. This iteration may unfold as spiraling if multivocal perspectives are accommodated. Thus, included within this focus are issues of how self-reference can inform methodologies and the research process in general.

Such self-analysis requires reflection and humility. Humility need not be self-deprecating, nor need it involve silencing the researcher's voice; research humility implies an awareness and sense of the unpredictability of the sociopolitical microcosm of the school and the changeable consequences of such reflexivity (Kincheloe and McLaren, 1994, p. 151). The challenge is to accommodate and transcend both the largely traditional mindsets within the school and the requirements of the Institute's Course Quality Assurance procedures and move to a critical realm of knowledge production and application. It is in organizing, disseminating, and interpreting information that the contribution to culinary arts education is made. The school, no longer caught as the passive receiver of "expert" knowledge becomes capable of generating and reflecting on its own knowledge and practices of the process, moving from the "is" to the "ought to be" by means of change, offering at the outset, possibilities but no certainties as to the outcomes of future events and not apparent prior to engaging in reflection-on-the-activity. The school learns to teach itself, learning both in and from the workplace, as part of the job. Reflexivity enables the identification and articulation of an educational philosophy, and encourages critical thinking in the sense that social life is reflective; that is, it has the capacity to change as our knowledge and thinking changes, thus creating new forms of social life which can, in their turn, be reconstructed (Carr and Kemmis, 1986).

The usual industry managerial "fix-it" approaches in which expedient solutions are sought for most situations, constrained by their immediacy, is severely challenged and forced by circumstances to change. The new approach concentrates on building "a learning community" and recognizes that the requirements for professionalism in culinary arts education needs to be created, particularly when such activity includes learning with colleague staff members through various staff development programs.

PROBLEM SOLVING OR CRITICAL THEORY IN CULINARY ARTS EDUCATION

Reflective methodology involves one in critical thinking in addition to developing problem-solving capabilities. Critical constructive thinking aims to improve the situation. The ways in which these capabilities are carried into curriculum theory were set out succinctly in Cox's (1980) well-known elaboration of the distinctions between problem-solving and critical theory:

Theory is always for someone and for some purpose. All theories have a perspective. Perspectives derive from a position in time and space. The world is seen from a standpoint definable in terms of national or social class, of dominance or subordination, of rising or declining power, of a sense of immobility or of present crisis, of past experience and of hopes and expectations for the future. Of course, sophisticated theory is never just the expression of a perspective. The more sophisticated a theory is, the more it reflects upon and transcends its own perspective, but the initial perspective is always contained within a theory and is relevant to its explication. There is, accordingly, no such thing as theory in itself, divorced from a standpoint in time and space. When any theory so represents itself, it is more important to examine it as ideology and to lay bare its concealed perspective . . .

Theory can have two distinct purposes. One is a simple, direct response to be a guide to help solve the problems posed within the terms of the particular perspective which was the point of departure. The other is more reflective upon the process of theorizing itself, to become clearly aware of the perspective which gives rise to theorizing and its relation to other perspectives (to achieve a perspective on perspectives), and to open up the possibility of choosing a different valid perspective from which the problematic becomes one of creating an alternative world. Each of these purposes gives rise to a different kind of theory. . . . The first purpose gives rise to problem-solving theory.

It takes the world as it finds it. With the prevailing social and power relationships and the institutions into which they are organized, as the given framework for action. The general aim of problem-solving is to make these relationships and institutions work smoothly by dealing effectively with particular sources of trouble. Since the general pattern of institutions and relationships is not called into question particular problems can be considered in to the specialized areas of activity in which they arise. Problem-solving theories are thus fragmented among a multiplicity of spheres or aspects of action, each of which assumes a certain stability in the other spheres (which enables them in practice to be ignored) when confronting a problem arising on its own. The strength of the problem-solving approach lies in its ability to fix limits or parameters to a problem area and to reduce the statement of a problem to a limited number of variables which are amenable to relatively close and precise examination. (p. 129)

In solving problems in culinary arts we seek to identify the cause of the problem and remove it, but this is not always possible and we end up analyzing a problem that more than likely, has been analyzed to death already. In such cases we begin to suffer the "paralysis of analysis." By contrast, the second purpose leads to critical theory.

Critical theory provides a stimulus to a new generation of culinary educators by combining dialectical methods to a new brand of committed analysis. This is critical in the sense that it stands apart from the prevailing order of the world and asks how that order came about. Critical theory, unlike problem solving, does not take institutions and social and power relationships for granted but calls them to question by concerning itself with their origins and how or whether they might be in the process of changing. It is directed toward an appraisal of the very framework for action, or problematic, which problem-solving theory accepts as its parameters. Critical theory is directed to the social and political complex as a whole rather than to the separate parts. As a matter of practice critical theory, problem-solving theory takes as its starting point some aspect or particular sphere of human activity (often described as Hegelian or humanist Marxism, whose revolutionary insights need to be preserved in constant dialogue, one with the other). But whereas the problem-solving approach leads to further analytic subdivision and limitation of the issues to be dealt with, the critical approach leads toward the construction of a larger picture of the whole of which the initially contemplated part is just one component, and seeks to understand the processes of change in which both parts and whole are involved (Cox, 1980, p. 130).

Critical theory is characterized by an interpretative approach combined with a pronounced interest in critically disputing actual social realities. It is sometimes referred to as critical hermeneutics. Its guiding principle is an emancipatory interest in knowledge. Thus, by combining practical and reflective activities, culinary arts educators may effectively combat the prevailing forces of domination. In this case, my interpretation of the curriculum development text for culinary arts replaced old preconceptions first by transforming my own schema or frames of reference. The curriculum development process was then connected to factors influencing its development, including team members' prior educational experience, their commitment to the process, professional experience, and other influences which would positively or negatively affect the text or its interpretation. Chapter 6 tells the story of the development of an undergraduate curriculum in culinary arts and opens the vista for further development.

Chapter 6

The Curriculum Journey

INTRODUCTION

This chapter tells the story of the culinary arts curriculum journey from initiation to validation, including its metamorphosis from a traditional craft-based vocational apprenticeship training paradigm, with its own modes of thinking, to a new paradigm in culinary arts inquiry which would be different and lead to the provision of a new integrated undergraduate degree curriculum.

The work of the school to date comprised:

- Certificate in Hotel and Catering Supervision (two years)
- Certificate in Culinary Arts (two years)
- Professional Chefs Apprentice Program over a year and sixteen weeks and on day release (two years full-time; three years day release)
- Professional Advanced Chefs programs (short/modular courses)
- Restaurant Service programs at Basic and Advanced levels (one year full-time; two years day release)
- Service-teaching provision to other schools in the College

THE CHRONOLOGY OF THE CURRICULUM DEVELOPMENT PROCESS (MAY 1996 TO MAY 1998)

The curriculum journey leading to a BA in Culinary Arts began formally on May 29, 1996. An inaugural meeting of all staff in the school was convened to discuss curriculum development in the context of a response to the mechanisms identified. Following a wide range of discussion the meeting proposed to pursue curriculum developments along the following lines: (1) a one-year diploma that would be open to culinary arts graduates and professional cookery graduates (provided the latter completed some form of bridging program to bring them up to speed); or (2) a three-year ab initio Diploma in Culinary Arts (McMahon, 1999).

The staff, in adopting the first of these proposals, sought to achieve two objectives: First, to respond to the demand from graduates of the Certificate in Culinary Arts for higher-level educational opportunities. Second, to formalize a higher-level award for a series of advanced cookery modules offered at the school under the auspices of the state training agency, the Council for the Education Recruitment and Training (CERT).

Another outcome of the inaugural meeting was the election of the chairman and secretary for the curriculum development team. Two additional staff members were coopted to assist the chairman and the secretary, and the head of the department became involved as a full member of the team, on his return from administrative service, in September 1996. However, two vital elements were missed, namely, the inclusion of student members and college administrators.

Following a new proactive approach to human resources development in the Institute the majority of staff members in the school were engaged in programs of self-development through study for primary and masters degrees or involved in research for doctoral degrees.

Curriculum Proposal (September 1996)

The preliminary proposal that emerged from the inaugural meeting was for a one-year add-on program, to the two-year certificate in culinary arts, to be titled Diploma in Culinary Arts. This was submitted to the Faculty Academic Board in September 1996 in accordance with the academic quality assurance procedures laid out in the Course Quality Assurance Handbook (1995, 1997), and discussed in Chapters 3 and 4. The proposal aimed at presenting a persuasive case to the authorities of the Institute and, eventually, to the Department of Education and Science, for the allocation of the resources necessary to run the program over the planned timescale. Desk-based research seeking to determine the characteristics of diploma programs offered in higher education institutes in the United States and Europe, including the United Kingdom, began at the inaugural meeting and continued throughout the summer months.

Developing Beliefs, Values, and Goals for the Program (October 1996 to January 1997)

At the beginning of the new 1996/1997 academic session, start of term activities in the school placed the usual heavy burden on the staff, such that little engagement with the curriculum development process was possible in the period October 1996 to January 1997. This burden was compounded by three extraneous events, namely, the appointment of a new director of the faculty, a proposed new structure for the faculty, and the absence of the department head during the month of December 1996. The status and future existence of the school in the context of the new appointment and the proposed new structure for the faculty became an issue for the school, because the school was excluded from the proposed new structure. This caused internal turmoil with lecturers driven in the face of unprecedented uncertainty to address and discuss hitherto unknown issues threatening both their own futures and that of the school. A series of meetings took place formally and informally in January and February 1997 around the questions: What are we in the school good at? How will we measure up in the new faculty? What are the academic areas within the school? Why are we and our work being ignored? (Aides minutes, January and February 1997).

These questions were arrived at through the well-known management technique of brainstorming. Brainstorming was used to facilitate creativity and to go beyond the school's conventional wisdom. The key value of the technique was that it allowed contributors to freewheel and to generate many ideas without fear of criticism. The "brainstorming" session held on January 24, 1997, was held in the absence of the department head because his position in the management hierarchy and his approach might inhibit the free flow of interaction usually found in unstructured situations. The brainstorming session was pivotal in the curriculum development process for the new program in culinary arts because some of the questions and ideas

arising during this session had never been asked before in the life of
the school. They included:

> What is culinary arts? What is industry doing at present? What
> is a Chef Manager? How would the program be marketed? Did
> naming the program before the ideas are developed narrow the
> focus? If this program had an academic base—did this mean
> Central Application Office (CAO) entry? What about people
> without CAO entry requirements? (Aides minutes, January 24,
> 1997)

These questions carried a set of hidden agendas and flagged tensions in the challenges to be faced, between the continuation of past
trade practices and the adoption of the new paradigm, that of developing a third-year program of study for a diploma in culinary arts. The
tension was increased by the expectation that those studying for the
diploma would achieve "management" level jobs through a "Diploma in Culinary Management."

The documentary research revealed a further set of seemingly in-
coherent questions and objectives continuing to be asked around:

> What results do we want to achieve? To equip students to . . . en-
> gage in applied problem-solving, . . . to analyze, . . . to study
> . . . . Move on from skill-based second year. Simulated situation;
> third year placement; involvement of industry—strengthen pro-
> fessional involvement in the course. Teaching staff—in-service
> training, team approach. (Aides minutes, January 24, 1997)

Answers were not found to most of the questions because of a lack
of "tractus" or theoretical background and a lack of conceptual capacity in the school. There was a gap in the school's ability to address
such questions in the abstract. Frustration added to the tension because culinary arts lecturers were always upbeat and sure about everything they did and how they perceived themselves, and were perceived by others in the faculty as being certain, in their (cooking)
roles began to encounter disciplinary vagueness. In the new circumstances, to seek help from colleagues in other schools would make
them appear vulnerable, add to their paranoia, and perhaps expose
them as not knowing as much as they credited themselves with. Criti-

cism of one's disciplinary expertise is very threatening and admitting frailty within the school could be interpreted as an actual admission of disciplinary vagueness, thereby increasing vulnerability, particularly, in light of the proposed curriculum development, the proposed faculty structure, and the apparent uncertain future of the school.

However, reflection on these issues helped to confirm that the staff in the school were prime movers, essential to the creation of the new curriculum, and prepared to adopt a new approach to professionalizing the culinary arts field. Old cookery myths and magic began with great difficulty to be deconstructed and attempts were made at reconstruction within the new paradigm as the first steps to progress toward professionalism and professionalization were taken. In addition, questions along the following lines continued to inhibit attempts to formulate aims and objectives for the program, because of their industry focus and instrumentality:

> Do we know how many employers expect to [employ] someone like we hope to produce? Many staff in restaurant industry in particular already who have no training. Where do graduates fit into industry? What other directions can they take? What is the overall aim of the new course? (Aides minutes, January 24, 1997)

Clearly the focus of the program objectives for a degree program needed to be different from the traditional "needs of industry" objectives, which had defined the craft-based apprenticeship programs to date.

Deciding Aims and Learning Outcomes (January to March 1997)

All the ideas identified in the brainstorming session were recorded and allowed to incubate, answers were arrived at slowly, over a series of meetings held between January and March 1997. The issues of aims and objectives, in particular, were reviewed and the learning and teaching strategies through which they would be achieved were discussed. The framing of these aims and objectives by the lecturers concerned was of signal importance to the curriculum development work in the school if the necessary change of focus was to be achieved.

The first statement of aims and objectives in the program proposal of September 1996 appeared to be both catch-all and instrumental. Nevertheless, as part of the iterative process the curriculum team began to realize that the focus, aims, objectives, and content would need to be "revisited again and again and again until agreement was reached." The reiterated aims and objectives improved on the original objectives presented in the program proposal and included:

- to develop a program of study for the needs of the individual working in the catering industry;
- to provide a basis for further study and motivation toward future career development;
- to achieve excellent understanding in application of fundamentals of cookery;
- to apply and understand how the use of this knowledge can be used in catering operations;
- to analyze the problems that may arise and to be aware how conflict can be used to good advantage;
- to understand that the menu is a marketing tool;
- to equip students with a high level of knowledge and skills so that she or he is confident and capable of taking a good level position in the food industry;
- to provide students with the practical and managerial skills to effectively operate at the top of their profession in the long term;
- to equip students with good culinary skills which are underpinned by high awareness of food science, food health and safety, and analytical ability.

As the curriculum development process continued, it became clear that simply adopting and adapting aims and objectives from other programs would not fit the requirements for the new program. Also, it emerged that lecturers designing the new curriculum needed to be clear on what they wanted students taking their subjects to learn. One outcome of these discussions was the recognition that four levels of aims and objectives needed to be addressed. These were: (1) the total holistic curriculum (including the hidden curriculum), (2) the subject, (3) the modules within a subject, and (4) the individual lesson (class).

For each of these categories it was necessary to distinguish aims and objectives, as each represented a different level of focus on a topic or problem area. The challenges were to recognize the total curriculum as one holistic integrated program, to state aims and objectives for the total curriculum, and then to cascade these objectives down to the individual lessons which would be delivered in a variety of classroom formats. The constraints on team members of their prior training and experience in professional cookery caused them some difficulty in focusing on the holistic totality of the curriculum. One such effect of these constraints was the emphasis on the acquisition of lower level application skills without knowledge or comprehension. These were promoted at the expense of higher order skills of analysis, synthesis, and evaluation (Bloom, Krathwohl, and Masia, 1956). Another was the use of the term "skills." This caused much confusion and some emotional reaction. Most members of the curriculum team and the wider school staff associated the term "skill" with knife skills and kitchen drills, for example "to turn a potato," rather than with conceptual, transferable, or critical-thinking skills. Nevertheless, these were the challenges to be overcome, opportunities afforded, and the team did not shirk in their endeavors to overcome them.

Framework for Moving Forward

A framework for moving forward was prepared by the curriculum team (see Figure 6.1). The first part presented the process the curriculum team had to work through, namely, aims, objectives, program content, implementation, and evaluation in order to begin preparing a program document. The second part comprised identifying influences that could affect the process, such as the verification of demand for the program, and the research necessary to underpin curriculum development, as well as to identify culinary arts content. The brainstorming session and subsequent meetings led the team to the realization of the necessity of moving from the certainty of craft-based vocational training to the uncertainty of a liberal vocational education. This was to become an essential feature in moving forward.

FIGURE 6.1. Framework for Moving Forward

Change of Design (March 1997)

The new faculty director, following a meeting with the team on March 11, articulated the view in a distinctively managerialist communication, that the work the curriculum team was engaged in did not comply with his preferred option for curriculum development. He instructed that, "the most appropriate course of action to take is to develop a design for the Diploma from year one" (Mulvey, 1997, p. 2). This intervention marked the rise of the new form of executive manipulation and a repudiation of established collegiality and academic autonomy in the Institute. It caused some concern and put further burdens of uncertainty and stress on the curriculum team, who felt that their work to date had gone down the tubes and that this was a tactic to discourage rather than support the proposed curriculum development. The director's communication contained a strong suggestion in favor of the team adopting a curriculum model from a sister program within the institute. This contributed to a deepening sense of oppression and paranoia hanging like a cloud over the school. There was both disappointment and annoyance, but little resistance to the proposed change because, as already noted, it had been logged as an option at the inaugural meeting in May 1996.

In addition, this change of emphasis was framed in the context of the Institute's newly found degree awarding powers and its pursuit of university status. Most significantly, the director's letter referred to a "longer-term development of a degree," a position later confirmed by the director of academic affairs when he advised the team that "the task of moving from a craft-based practice to a knowledge-based discipline for a diploma/degree course requires a holistic approach rather than an 'Add-on' to a certificate" (Gillingham, 1997). The effect of the directors' interventions was a further blow to the team's self-esteem and caused the enthusiasm for the culinary arts curriculum project to wane temporarily.

Nevertheless, the notion of developing an ab initio diploma/degree offered the curriculum team the opportunity to "rise again," and to become motivated and reinvigorated. This was fully supported and encouraged by the department head who interpreted the change in design positively and was proactive in availing of the opportunity to restore enthusiasm and raise morale within the school. The team addressed the implications of focusing on an ab initio diploma that, sometime in the future, would become a degree. During the meeting it was decided to skip the diploma and go directly to creating a degree in culinary arts. For the next few months, in order to maintain a framework for progress, the phrase diploma/degree was used in communications on the curriculum development process.

By May 1997, a draft Work in Progress Report, explicating the context for rethinking culinary arts education, was prepared and circulated to all staff in the school (Progress report, May 1997). This report portrayed the circularity, uncertainty, and difficulty on many fronts in tackling the designing and development of such a degree. There was no single meaning for the term culinary arts (let alone the term "curriculum"), or for example, no definitions of cook, chef, culinarian, or what was meant by the term "best culinary practice" in the new context. Different definitions emerged with each inquiry to serve different, mostly instrumental purposes, and the likelihood of an agreed definition remains problematic and an issue debated to this day. This debate is influenced particularly by the paradox of the industry's image which is one of low-paid, poorly motivated, and transient staff, often working in fear of their head chefs and restaurant managers, in a nonquality organization seeking to produce "quality" products. The role of the chef is recognized as demanding, stressful, and sheer hard work (Bates and Dunston, 1995; Bourdain, 2001). This realization brought the curriculum team round full circle almost to the beginning of the project, one year earlier, and faced them with the question: Would it ever be possible to design a degree course in culinary arts?

September 1997 to January 1998

At the start of the 1997/1998 academic session the proposed new structure for the faculty encountered some industrial relations problems. There was strong opposition from the teachers' union, and it became clear that no changes would take place without consultation with the union members affected. These industrial relations problems did not impede progress on the curriculum development and the second phase of the process began in September 1997.

Three dominant features of this phase were the growing internalization by the team of the breadth and depth of the curriculum development process, of the wealth of data generated both from their secondary and primary research and the publication of the Interim Report in January 1998. The chairman of the curriculum team issued an action plan for the months of September and October 1997 that included:

- Team Building/Program Development workshop for staff members participating in the Culinary Arts Curriculum Development Program;
- Industry Practitioners (Chefs) Focus Groups;
- Industry Management Focus Group;
- Graduates (and Others) Focus Group;
- Development of program framework;
- Preparation of the Interim Report required;

- Identifying a demand for the program;
- Preparation of curriculum aims and objectives;
- Outline program content based on the evidence of primary and secondary research;
- Program document;
- Implementation;
- Modularization;
- Assessment procedures;
- Validation; and
- Measurement and evaluation (Memorandum, September 1997).

Letters had been circulated to a random selection of executive and nonexecutive chefs, restaurant managers, hotel general managers, and catering managers, advising them that curriculum development was an ongoing curriculum activity in the school, and asking them for information on industry trends and their willingness to participate in the Culinary Arts curriculum development program.

In October 1997, primary research data included preliminary interviews with target groups including: recruitment agencies, equipment suppliers, group managing directors, chef patrons, head chefs, dieticians, and catering managers. These informants were identified from the aforementioned groups, as well as through personal contacts who had indicated their willingness to participate in the process. Interviews were informal, allowing participants to speak openly about their reactions to and expectations of the proposed culinary arts degree program. Three industry focus groups, each of twelve persons, constituted following Norton's (1985) advice, from those who responded to the letters of invitation. The membership of each focus group self-selected randomly according to their availability to attend on either of the days scheduled. These groups comprised Industry Practitioners (Chefs), October 1 and 2; Industry Management, October 3; and Professional Cookery Graduates, October 7. The focus groups were organized and facilitated by external professionals to ensure that the voices of all participants were heard.

Recurrent themes arising from the focus groups' data were: dissatisfaction with the current provision for culinary arts education, a strong indication of a need to develop culinary arts as a profession, and the demand for a degree level course in culinary arts. In addition, the focus group identified a range of subject areas for possible inclusion in the proposed culinary arts degree program including:

- Information technology;
- Environmental waste control;
- Hygiene, Health, and Food Safety;
- Leadership, communications, and people skills;
- Foreign language;
- Catering systems;
- Engineering and technology;
- Restaurant concept development and design;
- Entrepreneurial, financial, and business skills;
- Wine, oenology, and beverages; and
- Customer awareness.

Further, the data provided issues for consideration on some aspects of creating the learning environment by stating that learning be facilitated through such intangibles as theater, fun, and passion for food, its preparation, presentation, service, and consumption. The findings of the industry focus groups supported the curriculum development undertaken in the school and indicated that there was a real need for a three-year diploma/degree course to reflect the major trends in the culinary arts and that the range of approaches to teaching needs to be extended. Critical reflection at this point reveals the importance of establishing a theoretical base for the culinary arts curriculum because, simply to respond to the findings of the industry groups, while necessary at some level, would be an insufficient basis upon which to proceed from an educational perspective. Further research would be needed to develop the critical theory base for culinary arts.

Despite this caveat, in October 1997 the first steps in the design of culinary arts curriculum units were initiated, especially "culinary core" theory and practical units. All staff members were invited to make syllabus submissions in their specialist areas for inclusion in the proposed culinary arts diploma/degree program. An important staff meeting on October 30, 1997, discussed the draft working report and reflected on the findings of the industry focus groups. These included content areas to be considered for inclusion in the program, the staff's interest in developing subject materials, and preparations for compiling the interim report. A note to my diary shows that five staff members called in sick on that day. Nevertheless, this meeting was of great significance.

Most of the time was consumed in considering the findings of the draft working report and much discussion centered on questioning everything we do at present, assessing the purpose of higher liberal vocational education, and matching the feedback from industry to theoretical subjects. The draft working report highlighted six key areas discussed in the focus groups, namely:

> *Key Area 1:* Historical experiences in the school, both positive and negative;
>
> *Key Area 2:* The Present: strengths, weaknesses, opportunities and threats (SWOT) analysis;
>
> *Key Area 3:* The Future: requirements for the culinary profession;
>
> *Key Area 4:* Bridging the gap with appropriate capacities and capabilities;
>
> *Key Area 5:* Opportunities that could enable progress in culinary arts education; and
>
> *Key Area 6:* Obstacles that could inhibit such progress.

The focus groups' key areas contributed to clarifying many of the essentials required for the program aims, content, and structure.

Following the team's research and meetings held during November and December 1997 a decision to prepare a draft Interim Report was made in order to consolidate and coordinate all the curriculum development activities and to gather them in one formal document. In December 1997 the "draft Interim Report on the Development and Structure of the proposed course leading to a Bachelor's Degree in Culinary Arts" was circulated for information and comment to all colleagues in the school.

Interim Report (January 1998)

The Interim Report, claimed as the first attempt at a scholarly review of culinary arts education in Ireland, was presented to the Faculty Academic Board in January 1998. It was strongly welcomed by the Faculty Academic Board, and the faculty director who as chairman of the Faculty Academic Board approved the development of the program document, and urged wider dissemination and publication. As a result, in the period January to May 1998, the preparation of the program document took on a new urgency and passed through various iterations that will be further elaborated below.

The major conclusion of the research to date was that a broader knowledge-based education to degree level needed to be provided that would prepare students to take up careers in culinary arts. The Interim Report 1998 presented new insights into the culinary arts education scene even though both the "technical literature" for culinary arts and "evaluative studies" designed to inform policy and practice for culinary arts' industrial and vocational training purposes was sparse. The data flowing from the industry focus groups combined with developments in the Institute created an unprecedented demand for the establishment of an undergraduate degree program in this new field. Further, pressure for the development of the new program was created by the wave of emotion and enthusiastic support within the school and the faculty.

Program Philosophy, Aims, Outcomes, Content, and Structure

The philosophy, aims and outcomes, content and structure for the proposed curriculum were informed by the findings of the Interim Report (1998). For the first time, the philosophy that cookery would be taught as every subject is taught at the undergraduate level, that is, "in academic alignment" (Rietz, 1961, p. 21) and on the basis of complete exposition from a historical foundation to contemporary development (Goodson, 1998, pp. 13-18) became realizable.

The curriculum team insisted on maintaining, as one of its major objectives, that students should be "able to cook." This remains an interesting and contested objective, the exact meaning of which remains to be successfully defined. However, in the interests of making progress, the view that the development of an aesthetic approach, in which all previous relationships between culinary arts and the expression of direct aesthetic awareness would be transformed, was taken.

Culinary arts in its gastronomic context would no longer serve as a metaphor for the arts but would assume its rightful place among them. Students would be encouraged toward independent self-learning and culinary idiosyncrasy, challenging the orthodoxy of the recipe. The notion of developing the student's knowledge in an autonomous way may seem on the one hand attractive, in that individuals can pursue that which interests them. The challenge was to facilitate learning, to explore the science and psychology behind the gastronomic event, and to prepare students for a professional practice that requires knowledgeable, safe, and capable professional practitioners preparing, cooking, and serving food and beverages to the public in a variety of settings. However, the concept of independent study is valid if it is regarded as predominantly a self-regulating mode of broadening students' knowledge and skills, leading to the acceptance of the highest ethical standards in practice. It was agreed, at a succession of curriculum team and staff meetings in January and February 1998, that a broader, intellectual approach to Culinary Arts needed to be adopted. This meant recognizing the disciplines from which subjects, such as Culinary Arts Principles and Practices, Gastronomy, and Life Sciences derived. These derivations would form the core elements of the program. Around these would be drawn the articulation of arts (aesthetics), business and enterprise, life sciences technology, and languages. The proposed program structure was debated at length and with some intensity at another pivotal, dynamic, and externally facilitated meeting on January 29, 1998. At this meeting, the issue of lecturers' class contact hours, accommodations, and resources to offer their courses were among the subjects most hotly debated. Each subject teacher expressed the view that his or her subject required at least twenty hours per week to teach. In this school, thirty-three hours class contact per week was not uncommon. The expectation was that the new culinary arts degree program would be offered within a norm of eighteen to twenty-four hours per week initially, reducing to twelve hours per week in the later years in order to develop independent student learning (Memorandum, February 6, 1998).

Subject teams were identified and comprised a minimum of four persons, except the Culinary Arts team, which had fifteen names registered. There was some cross-membership. This was considered essential in the attempt to structure a holistic curriculum.

As the work progressed, aims and learning outcomes were developed and agreed by the various subject teams and put in place to progress the development of the curriculum process and focus on specific aspects of the curriculum. The concepts deriving from the focus groups and related investigations coincided with the breadth and depth of knowledge identified by the curriculum team for this program. Students would develop the knowledge and skills necessary for the selection, combination, cooking, presentation, and service of safe food through the study of Culinary Arts; Life Sciences; IT/Technology; Enterprise; Art and Aesthetics; Languages; and Professional Internship. These were to be clustered into four pillars of learning with the following aims and learning outcomes:

- to develop a program of study for the needs of the individual working in the catering industry;
- to provide a basis for further study and motivation toward future career development;
- to achieve excellent understanding in application of (artistic and scientific) fundamentals of cookery;
- to apply and understand how the use of this knowledge can be used in culinary arts operations;
- to analyze the problems that may arise and to be aware how conflict can be used to good advantage;
- to understand that the menu is a marketing tool, and a production blueprint;
- to equip students with a high level of knowledge and skills so that they become confident and capable of taking a good level position in the food industry;
- to provide students with the practical and managerial skills to effectively operate at the top of their profession in the long term;
- to equip students with culinary skills that are underpinned by high awareness of food science, food hygiene and safety, and analytical capability.

Four "Pillars" of Learning (February/March 1998)

In the penultimate phase of the curriculum process these subject areas were identified, clustered, and formed into four elements or "pillars" of learning, to be worked on by disciplinary teams. The four elements are illustrated as follows:

Information Technology	Culinary Arts	Food and Life Sciences	Business and Enterprise
Information	Gastronomy	Food science	Accountancy
Technology	Performing restaurants arts	Microbiology and hygiene	Management
Hardware and software	Language	Health and safety	Marketing
Information systems	Art and design	Physiology	Managing change
Communications technology	Culinary arts major	Nutrition	Innovation
Catering systems	Gastronomic experience	Food safety	Enterprise
Computers and equipment	Table arts	Lifestyle	New products development
	Customer care		Professional internship
	New product design		

The guiding philosophy of the BA in Culinary Arts was to move beyond the utilitarian and traditional task-based, craft-apprenticeship tradition in professional cookery toward a more academic and scholarly approach that reflected high status, academic and practical (liberal-vocational) knowledge, thereby improving culinary arts education. A seminar titled Mechanics of Curriculum Development, held on February 27, 1998, reinforced the team's need to develop the intellectual capacity of students, rather than to instill the wrist-to-fingertip drills of the traditional approach, and to maximize the potential of each individual student to carve out for herself or himself a worthwhile life in the broad field of food-related careers.

Curriculum activity during the period March to May 1998 was frenzied and often seemed disorganized, as a number of activities were taking place in parallel. Issues such as the availability of facilities, secretarial assistance or meeting rooms became highly emotive; disagreements arose on the relative importance of certain subjects; who was going to teach which subjects; whether outside service

teaching would be required or whether staff were sufficiently qualified to teach in this program. Issues of curriculum content, staff and
class timetables, contact hours, teaching methods, estimated student
workload, schedules, structure, and weighting of each examination
were all vigorously contested, as were the assessment and examination marks and standards and regulations for progression.

Lecturers, while committed to the new program, experienced some
difficulty in internalizing the requirements for an undergraduate degree program in a way that would not only make it their own, but
would enable them to develop it further. The literature pointed to the
observation that teachers sometimes have it in their power to take
control of the curriculum but do not know how to go about it (Lawton,
1998, p. 22, cited in McCulloch et al., 2000, p. 13). "Territorial" demands by various groups and individual lecturers further illustrated
this difficulty. For example, life sciences lecturers demanded a six-
week immersion course in the fundamentals of science (physics and
chemistry), culinary arts teachers wanted to include a foundation
course in culinary science, but insisted that students get into the kitchen
to commence cooking immediately in order to satisfy unsubstantiated
student expectations. The enterprise and business group sought an additional module of learning to learn as a prerequisite to their courses.
The gastronomy group wanted an introduction to anthropology and sociology prior to engaging with gastronomy itself. The range of ideas
within the syllabi led to considerable overlap, and there was clearly a
need for consolidation and integration. That is, linkages had to be established and have a logical coherence that was clear to the lecturers,
before they could make them clear to the students. Whether this was
finally achieved remains a matter of conjecture.

In the team meetings, debate focused both on how students would
learn how to learn and on what they ought to be taught. Practical
cookery and food service lecturers tended to focus on the practical
performance of manual (psychomotor) skills to the virtual exclusion
of theoretical knowledge. Life sciences lecturers agreed that the fundamentals of science were holistic and to attempt to apply such knowledge without a reasonable understanding of analysis and evaluation
skills would be mistaken. Discussions continued until everyone present came to realize that if all the contact hours deemed essential were
facilitated, there would not be sufficient time in the four years to offer

the pre-year of the program. The notion that preceding gastronomy, enterprise, and business courses with full courses in sociology and psychology, or preceding the life sciences with full courses in biology, chemistry, and physics was clearly revealing, but was not likely to be feasible. Nevertheless, without certain basic concepts from these disciplines the treatment of these areas would be shallow, descriptive, and based on uncritical current practice. The myth of the task-based operative in the kitchen was likely to be perpetuated.

The problem was to determine if it were possible, from the discussions, to develop certain problem-based concepts and create opportunities for students through their own learning, to encourage problem-based learning and critical thinking skills. These intellectual activities are the same whatever the problem. The fundamental modes of thinking must be developed within and between the different subjects in the curriculum. Nonetheless, the focus of the team and the wider staff remained fixed on the number of teaching hours available for their program. Most of the lecturers became very upset if the hours they sought for their subjects were not made available. They argued that any reduction in class contact time by "management" meant a reduction in the quality of the program. All the demands for class contact hours and subject territory increased with each syllabus submission. The head of the department feared for the curriculum. He was aware, also, that the successful implementation of the program could have profound consequences for the school, since students would be able to participate on the program committee, engage with the curriculum on the basis of their experiences, and articulate their own views on its implementation.

Diagrams depicting pathways of the program through each of the years and the relationships of subjects were put up on flip charts. These were drawn, withdrawn, and redrawn. Subject details, including rationale and relevance to overall program, and integration with other components were constant companions during the later period of the program document preparation, with each viewpoint attempting to hold its own ground, often emotionally rather than rationally. The impending Validation Event, looming ever closer, generated additional pressure.

The level of lecturer's intransigence proved much more difficult than anticipated. Tensions between the craft-based vocational training people and the liberal education people, in particular, attempting to reconcile the utilitarian advantages of "doing" subjects with the intellectual aspirations of "studying" the discipline which, up to this point, were largely internal began to surface publicly. Lecturers experienced both the paradoxical challenge of becoming professional educators and dealing with the significant role of emotions in their work. Hargreaves (as cited in McCulloch et al., 2000, p. 115) tells us that "if teachers want to become professionally stronger, they must open themselves up and become more publicly vulnerable and accessible." This concept was foreign to culinary arts lecturers in the school, and was perceived as a threat to their "status."

With only a month to the Validation Event a note in the head of the department's diary expressed a panicked concern that the curriculum development process was in danger of floundering. "Curriculum team in total disarray. They seem never to tire from stepping into self-generated black holes" (Diary entry, April 20, 1998).

In an attempt to meet the deadline for the validation event, syllabi were sought from the other schools in the Faculty who had expertise in aspects of the curriculum not available at the appropriate level within the school. Such a move received reluctant approval from the curriculum team and lecturers in the school. Although there was some evidence of movement away from the craft-based approach by members of the culinary arts subject team, most lecturers continued to insist on their claims to privilege "practical cookery skills."

Learning, Teaching, and Assessment in Culinary Arts

Learning and teaching methodologies in culinary arts were expected to reflect and inform the principles of the subject itself, by attending to the ways in which students develop their knowledge and understanding, their application of key principles to related contexts, their ability to reflect on salient issues, and their development of transferable skills. It was agreed that these would not be treated as discrete or separate aspects of culinary arts, but would cohere to form a unified discipline. Therefore, an understanding that learning, teaching, and assessment needed to be closely interrelated, and be seen as student related, began to be acknowledged by the team.

Approaches to assessment likewise would be expected to support student learning, and the content contributing to that learning. In particular, students would be required to undertake a range of appropriate methods of assessment, deriving from the teaching and learning approaches and methodologies within the individual pillars. In that sense learning, teaching, and assessment would be interrelated in line with the philosophy of the curriculum.

Learning and teaching. Apart from the difficulty with syllabi, tensions arose between the demands of the more theoretical aspects of the program and the raising of the practical aspects to a more conceptually demanding level than the traditional cooking "drill" of the apprenticeship programs. Teaching and learning methods were aimed at encouraging independent study and learning. The student was seen as the key participant in her or his own learning (Program Document, 1998, p. 26). Students were to be encouraged to actively engage in their own learning by means of attendance at lectures, tutorials, discussions, debates, seminars, field visits, visiting lecturers, professional internship, research, reflection, and presentation. Where appropriate, students' specific objectives and expectations were stated, particularly, in relation to learning skills to be acquired through professional internship.

Timetabling was envisaged as needing to become more flexible, with time allotted for self-directed learning. Timetables, more often than not, prevent the development of learning and teaching strategies aimed at best achieving the objectives set. In undergraduate education timetables are based on the lecture. Little flexibility is permitted despite all the work on the ineffectiveness of lectures. There was an additional difficulty in the school because lecturers were accustomed to "passing on 'my' knowledge" in the form of a practical/didactic method over thirty hours student contact per week. Timetabled teaching hours, in the proposed program, were allocated in consultation with the subject lecturers but these remain vehemently contested because of lecturers' demand for maximum contact hours to "teach" their subjects. This is a weakness in the program that will take a little more time to address.

The curriculum content area causing most anxiety was the "culinary core," in particular the "practical." Traditionally, practical work in culinary arts generally involved "cooking, making dishes and doing" under instruction from a teacher. Such approaches to practical cookery teaching have been criticized by Rietz (1961) and McGee

(1992) as teaching without formal educational processes. Cookery by such means is taught as a craft. The bases of instruction are almost entirely restricted to operating techniques. Nevertheless, practical work has traditionally established itself into a very influential position in teaching culinary arts in many countries. The culinary core, in this case, was represented as a "unique educational experience" for students in the program.

In most learning and teaching situations students are involved in reading, writing, listening, and talking. However, in studying cookery (culinary core) and table arts students are involved in subjects that take place in both kitchen and dining areas of a restaurant. Practical cookery and restaurant service classes may be similar to practical work in science. Students work with their hands, they weigh and measure, they plan their work, and they produce dishes and prepare the dining room for service. Practical work in science generally means engaging the intellect by carrying out experiments with scientific apparatus, usually in a science laboratory (Kennedy, 1998, p. 117). In cookery, students carry out instructions or follow written recipes to produce various uncritical versions of a "dish." Similar to science students, cookery students work in a more relaxed atmosphere in a spirit of cooperation where they help each other but they do not always work as part of a team. Thus, in practical work, science students encounter ideas and verify principles firsthand, that is, a type of "hands-on" learning, and culinary arts students follow uncritically the didactic instructions of their teachers. On reflection, new methods to teach practical culinary arts need to be created, and the means by which lecturers can be encouraged to participate in team-teaching, experimental cookery, and teaching cookery through multimedia all need further research.

Assessments and examinations. Historically, staff members in the school developed their own means of assessing students' performance. Whether an individual lecturer employed any method to establish the validity and reliability of their assessment procedures was not known because there was reluctance by lecturers to submit these to colleagues for systemic or continuous review. Generally, there are no systematic attempts to compare students' performance across a number of subjects apart from the revelations of the examinations board meeting. No attempt was made either to predict students' future performance in the workplace. Assessment in the culinary arts program was concerned with whether students had achieved the aims and objectives of the professional cookery program, namely to prepare an already rehearsed menu in three hours. The measurement of students' capability involved a variety of approaches ranging from continuous assessment during the year to a terminal examination on completion of each year of the program (Program Document, 1998, p. 32). The inclusion of both formative and summative assessment methods in the new curriculum indicated the curriculum team's commitment to assisting the individual to learn at her or his own pace while still achieving some level of standards. Difficulties were envisaged in assessing both culinary core and communications skills and the notion of self- and peer-assessment was raised as possible solutions. These were seen as important in fostering the development of autonomous practitioners who would be able, for the first time, to take responsibility for monitoring their own standards of professional practice. Further work to establish marks and standards for the various subjects in the program continued. In the end, the assessment and examination regulations and the marks and standards of the Institute were used for the program validation event, and the debate on examination and assessment continues.

Professional Internship

Much discussion took place on the value of professional internship as a component of the program. Many staff were adamant that industrial experience was essential. An alternative view was that if professional internship were to be included in the program it could not follow the traditional pattern of sending students blindly into industry as "fodder." The question of industrial placement's contribution to the students' "learning" required much more consideration than the time available would allow. Learning in work placement requires experience coupled with reflective, structured approaches to facilitate the student in developing her or his thinking abilities. Professional internship was envisaged for short periods in years 1 and 2 in Ireland, with an international exchange in year 3 to allow students to increase their confidence, both in professional and language capabilities. The duration of the professional internship, originally ten weeks, was reduced, under severe protest from the team, to eight weeks, to enable the students as unpaid supernumeraries to enjoy the long summer vacation available to most other students. This was the first time that industrial practice for culinary arts students was unpaid and did not last the whole summer vacation. However, the concept of unpaid supernumeraries in professional internship was agreed to, only reluctantly, to enable the students to familiarize themselves with the world of work and practice skills, which would be "signed off" by industry practitioners, without the pressure on students of having to staff restaurants.

Submission to Faculty Academic Board Subcommittee (March 1998)

The Faculty Academic Board established a subcommittee to review documentation and assess whether the program was appropriate for submission to the validation panel. It identified a number of weaknesses. Although it recognized that the team had undertaken wide-ranging research, all the conclusions that might have been drawn and recommendations ensuing therefrom were not evident. The Faculty Academic Board Subcommittee deduced from the information provided that the program leaned too heavily toward applied management and was contrary to the stated aims to educate in the area of culinary arts. These were serious criticisms.

The Faculty Academic Board Subcommittee raised fourteen critical issues from the documentation submitted. Two of these included: to distinguish between certificate, diploma, and degree level work in culinary arts, and to document the justification of why the school could be the host school for this degree. The DIT Course Quality Handbook (1997, p. 121) sets out clear definitions for each category of course program certificate, diploma, and degree offered within the Institute.

The remainder of the fourteen critical issues raised by the Faculty Academic Board Subcommittee are synopsized as follows:

- specification of integrating mechanisms between subjects and pillars with emphasis on integrating subjects;

- account to be taken of students' capability of further study at graduate level;
- reduce hours in first year;
- develop fourth year to degree level;
- develop ability to research, for independent thought and cumulative knowledge; provide electives in fourth and possibly third years;
- widen the subject area in food; identify journals, books, CD-ROMs, and other media resources to underpin culinary arts program at degree level;
- discuss with other department heads;
- advised the team to follow the Course Quality Assurance procedures and submit Interim Report and whatever other documents approved by subcommittee in fulfillment of Academic Council's Quality Assurance requirements (correspondence, Faculty Board Subcommittee, March 19, 1998).

This report was circulated to all lecturers in the school. Despite these criticisms, the subcommittee supported the progression of the curriculum toward validation. Work on the syllabi continued apace. Supplementary information was prepared. The Faculty Academic Board Subcommittee instructed that the Quality Assurance Committee be advised that supplementary documents including comments from the Faculty Academic Board Subcommittee were on the way, and would be available in due time for the Validation Event. It focused the curriculum team on issues to be urgently actioned, rather than debated, and it presented them with an agenda for forward progress. Enthusiasm for the program within the Faculty remained high.

Easter Vacation 1998

During the Easter vacation members of the curriculum team engaged in a pragmatic and expeditious revision of the program document in order to respond positively to the criticisms of the Faculty Academic Board Subcommittee. They needed a more comprehensive and coherent program document to be available for colleagues, when revising and completing their individual syllabi following their Easter vacation on April 20. Members of the curriculum team prepared some syllabi, for example, Gastronomy, Culinary Arts Major, and the

Gastronomic Event in final year. Other syllabi, for example, Languages (French and German), Applied Food Science, and Accounting, were prepared by colleagues in the School of Hospitality and Tourism Management. On April 17, every staff member was posted a draft of the penultimate edition of the Program Submission. Attention was drawn to the requirement for the final corrected edition of the program document to go to the printer three days after their return, on April 23, 1998. A template for uniform presentation of syllabi was provided as a guide for staff to revisit their syllabi submissions. Their attention was particularly drawn to the Academic Board's critical review and on the need to formulate the Rationale, Overview of Subject areas, and Linkages; electives were considered and agreed; professional internship was reviewed and agreed.

Time pressure to produce the syllabi was extreme, and the process seemed at times to be floundering. Even though terms like "higher level" and "advanced" were frequently used, confidence in the understanding of the meanings or their rigorous application was difficult to discern. The demand by lecturers for ever more time, to enable students to understand "my subject" was argued as the basis for students having to have content before they could reflect on anything, and this had to be taught; therefore the slogan "we need our hours" prevailed. The block of hours allocated are presented in Table 6.1.

Composition of the Validation Panel

The Institute's Academic Council, in consultation with the Faculty Academic Board, is responsible for constituting the validation panel. The validation panel includes both internal and external peers familiar with current theory, practice, and developments in the relevant disciplines, independent of the school or faculty proposing the program and some of whom are independent of the institute (DIT Quality Assurance Handbook, 1997, pp. 37, 38).

Also, it is desirable that members should possess an understanding of teaching, learning, assessment, and examination work in higher education, be familiar with similar institutions and have an awareness of the general requirements for academic awards at the level proposed for the new program. The validation panel comprised:

- three persons from inside the institute including the chairperson: a senior academic from a faculty not involved in offering the program (in this case, the Head of School of Chemistry); a member with particular responsibility for quality assurance (in this case, the Head of School of Retail Services Management); and at least one staff member from the faculty, but not the school involved with proposing the program (in this case, the Head of School of Hospitality and Tourism Management).
- two external members nominated by the Faculty, one a senior academic in the discipline (in this case, Associate Vice-President for degree programs at the Culinary Institute of America) and a senior professional or industrial practitioner in a related discipline (in this case, the Group Managing Director for Corporate Human Resources and University Partnership of ACCOR, France).

TABLE 6.1. Hours Allocated for Course by Subject

Subject	Course Hours			
	Year 1	Year 2	Year 3	Year 4
Enterprise/Business Communication	3	4	2	
Enterprise/Product Innovation				3
Culinary Arts Core/ Gastronomy	12	13	6	
Gastronomic Event				3
Life Sciences	6	5	3	
Culinary Arts Major				3
Technology	2	2		
Product Development			2	
Languages	3	3	3	
Dissertation				3

Source: Program document, 1998, pp. 32-35.

In line with an Academic Council recommendation, external panel members should have no recent connection with the Institute. Neither of the external members in this case had had any previous connection with the Institute. They were nominated for their commitment to higher professional education in culinary arts and for their international reputation as leaders in the field. A senior member of the academic staff, independent of the faculty involved, was nominated to act as secretary and organizer of the validation panel.

The Validation Event (May 1998)

The Validation Panel is required to make an impartial judgment on the standard, content, and conduct of the proposed program and its comparability with other programs in Ireland and internationally. In order to inform its judgment, the Validation Panel visits the school to consider the program documentation, to discuss the proposed program with the program committee and with students and graduates of the school, and to view the facilities available to the program (DIT Quality Assurance Handbook, 1997, p. 35).

The Validation Event for the BA in Culinary Arts was originally scheduled for May 7 and 8, but the head of the department sought a deferral to prepare the team more adequately for the presentation of the Course Document to the Validation Panel. The Validation Event was rescheduled for May 28 and 29. This rescheduling gave the school time to better "know the document" and each lecturer to know their particular section of it, and also, to relate their section to the whole. The team prepared the first iteration of the what, why, and how of the development of the curriculum in culinary arts which was distributed to all staff on May 7. It described how the culinary arts curriculum was developed through a comprehensive process that included:

- school meetings to discuss potential development of the program;
- selection of curriculum development team;
- accumulation of secondary research;
- program model proposals and alternatives;

- primary research—discussions with key individuals in industry; academia, alumni, representative bodies, and colleague members of faculty;
- preparation of Interim Report, 1998;
- feedback and refining of subject proposals;
- selection of interdisciplinary teams;
- the development of rationale, aims and objectives, content, teaching and learning strategies, and methods of assessment and examination;
- preparation of draft Program Document;
- presentation to Faculty Academic Board; and
- preparation of final Program Document for presentation to Validation Panel.

In the weeks leading to the Validation Event the interdisciplinary teams were constantly engaged in revision, reiteration, and renewal of the material and in rehearsal for the presentations. All the staff of the school participated in the Validation Event. Each member of the curriculum development team was allocated the task of fielding questions from the panel in particular areas and advised to spread the response to colleagues for a more comprehensive explanation and at the same time exhibit an esprit de corps within the school.

The timetable of the validation event for the BA in Culinary Arts extended over a half of one day and one whole day, with a preliminary private meeting of the panel commencing at 2:30 p.m. on the first day, May 28, 1998. Between 3:00 and 6:00 p.m. the panel members were introduced to the director of the faculty, senior staff from the department, chairperson of the program committee, and the secretary of the program committee. The panel visited the facilities available to the program and privately reviewed in detail the documentation submitted. They discussed matters to be raised at subsequent meetings with various groups. The panel, the faculty director, and members of the department staff completed the first stage with an informal meeting over dinner. This meal was essentially a gastronomic event, the center of the commensality of the occasion. It was an opportunity for the panel to experience the work of the school in relation to culinary arts and the school availed itself of this opportunity enthusiastically.

On the following day, May 29, 1998, the panel met early in the morning to finalize procedures for the various meetings. The first meeting was with the curriculum team to discuss matters raised during the panel's private discussions, and arising from the program document particularly with the broader aspects of the program philosophy, its rationale, and issues of administration. The curriculum team was given permission to make a short presentation to the panel of the chronology of the curriculum development process, philosophy, aims, and linkages. This presentation was professional and it was well received. A member of the panel suggested that "we don't need to ask any more questions now." Following the presentation, the chairman invited members of the Validation Panel to interrogate the document and the process.

A range of questions arose around issues: why a trade or technical school would want to pursue a degree program in a field where there were no other such programs, how the school saw the difference between a craft apprenticeship program and the proposed degree program, and concerns about academic drift. The industry expert was fully enthusiastic about the program. The director of the Culinary Institute of America questioned the team as to the inclusion of the amount of science, information technology and languages to, in his opinion, the detriment of culinary core. The head of the department, fielding as instructed, responded that in order to gain academic recognition there was a tendency to move toward the conceptual and cognitive, that is, the higher stages of Bloom's Taxonomy (Bloom, Krathwohl, and Masia, 1956). This response did not please the questioner who retorted that, "You should take care not to parade in spurious clothing." The registrar spoke of the need to be proud of the course and stated that there was no need to dress it up in academic garb. The representative of the Quality Assurance Committee, among others, identified the staff's enthusiasm as palpable. He stated that he never before witnessed such enthusiasm at a Validation Event in the Institute.

The panel met in succession with some current students in the school and with graduates of the school to get an impression of how students felt about the quality of the courses they attended. After lunch, the panel met with staff lecturing in the program to discuss particulars of aims and objectives, syllabus, teaching and learning methods, and assessment issues. Unfortunately, no verbatim minutes of individual contributions were available, save a response from one impetuous staff member, who had little prior involvement with the team, to a question from the panel as to whose idea this program was. He jumped to his feet and yelled "'T' was mine!" (Diary entry, May 29, 1998).

Report on Validation Event

The main findings of the validation event, namely, the recommendation that the program be approved as a four-year honors degree in Culinary Arts with the usual range of classifications (Validation Panel, 1998, p. 4), were advised informally to the faculty director, department head, and chairperson of the program committee, on that day.

The Validation Panel identified two issues, namely the lack of academic qualifications of the staff to teach an honors degree program, and the limited facilities within which the proposed program would be offered. Further, the validation panel identified a number of weaknesses with the program documentation, and required a revised program document, ensuring accuracy and consistency in both content and style, to be resubmitted no later than October 31, 1998.

Specifically, the panel required a clearly expressed staff recruitment and development plan to demonstrate that "properly qualified and experienced staff, appropriate for an honors degree program of this type, are in place" (Validation Report, 1998, p. 5). Also, the panel insisted that staff must possess the knowledge, experience, and pedagogical skills necessary for a program that combines academic rigor with practical capabilities, even though not all need to be qualified at doctoral level. The panel made several further recommendations, the first of which was to continue to improve facilities available to the program. Specifically, that a technical laboratory, properly staffed by technicians, be attached to a production kitchen in order to facilitate the use of technology in the culinary area; that better office accommodations be provided to match teaching and research needs, together with a student lounge to facilitate interaction. Also, it recommended careful monitoring of the quality of internship locations and the quality of the learning experience. The Validation Panel required, in compliance with the Institute's Marks and Standards, that charts of assessment methodologies be made clear, consistent, and accurate.

These should match syllabi and subject titles. There should be a good rationale for each subject syllabus and relationships between subjects should be clearly expressed, as should the place of each subject in the program as a whole. Each subject should have appropriate teaching and learning strategies. The panel determined that course sequences and interrelationships be reviewed and clarified for each "theme" of the program together with the integration of each year and the program as a whole. The validation report was clear that culinary arts programs needed [industry] placements to ensure that students developed a full range of culinary arts and production skills and that these skills were identified and made explicit.

The report was forwarded to the Academic Council, and to the Governing Body for final approval and the imprimatur of the Institute (DIT Quality Assurance Handbook, 1995, 1997, p. 128). The approved program, consisting of a revised program document, corrected and modified to include all the conditions and recommendations stipulated by the validation panel, was completed by the due date, October 31, 1998. Copies of the approved Program Document were made available to the director of the faculty and the head of the department. They were lodged in the faculty library prior to the scheduled commencement of the program (Program Document, 1998).

In early September 1999, the head of the department was advised by the DIT's Admissions office that 340 Leaving Certificate points would be the entry level for the BA in Culinary Arts (Admissions Office, 1999). This was highly significant because the degree in Hospitality (Hotel and Catering) Management, which had been running in the college since the mid-1970s registered only ten points higher at 350. Thirty-three students accepted the first round offers to candidates. An additional call to achieve the target of forty-five was made by the admission office. On Monday September 20, 1999, thirty-eight students presented themselves for their first class (School Register, 1999).

CONCLUSION

Education as a social phenomenon is embedded in policy, political, and social contexts, inseparable triplets in education, as in any other sphere, where national and social interests are perceived (McCulloch,

1986, p. 35). The form of curriculum and its development could hardly have avoided challenging the status quo. In practice, different educational interests were favored or disfavored depending on the perceptions of the various players and on how the new reality was represented and interpreted. Thus, the hermeneutics and the theoretical assumptions were not neutral or value free but were part of, and helped to construct, the political and ideological conditions necessary to overcome inertia and opposition (Alvesson and Skoldeberg, 2000, p. 8).

Clearly, reflection on such involvement in the wider arena required that the participants recognize that they were working in a political context, where curriculum development was embedded in creative tension between challenging the existing social order (status quo) or accepting and reproducing or reforming and improving it. The latter might be said to have been achieved, to a greater or lesser extent.

Reflection on documentary material underpinning this curriculum journey revealed how slow progress was in getting the curriculum development process for culinary arts under way. The framework presented in Chapters 3 and 4 aimed to illustrate a process, structure, and direction for addressing curriculum development. It is likely that the appropriateness or otherwise of any model or combination of models means that some parts are rejected and others are included, thereby creating a new model that leads through critical reflection toward continuous improvement.

It is clear from the research data that, at the beginning of the process, the school was not sophisticated and it could be considered to have been academically naive, although it was emotionally charged. The claim that this curriculum journey developed a program that offers individual students opportunities to become expert, scientific, and caring professionals (Program Document, 1998, p. 17) will be substantiated only after a number of cohorts have completed the program and a tradition of scholarly work in the discipline emerges, along with a corps of trained specialists from which lecturers and researchers may be recruited. This curriculum journey has shown that the curriculum development process contributed many positive changes to both the subject/discipline and within the school. It is suggested that a much more reflective atmosphere is evident in the school, as most members of staff have completed degrees, at either bachelor's, master's, or doctoral level since the beginning of the curriculum development process. In addition, staff recruitment at master's or doctorate level is a more regular phenomenon in the school.

It will be clear from this account of the curriculum journey that a spirit of dynamism rather than one of mechanistic obedience toward prescription was the driving factor. Mechanistic obedience would have been fatal to the development and implementation of the curriculum. Curriculum development needs to be undertaken by the program team. Lecturers deprived of freedom, initiative, and responsibility cannot fulfill their educational functions except by depriving their students of these same vital qualities. Given the time span for this culinary arts curriculum development process and the lack of conceptual capability and curriculum development experience in the school at the beginning of the process, it is clear that the transformation of the culture within the school, although a struggle, has been dramatic.

Chapter 7

Assuring Curriculum Quality in Graduate Diplomas and Master's Degrees in Culinary Arts and Gastronomy

Creating graduate diplomas and master's degrees in culinary arts and gastronomy is currently an innovative notion for the higher education establishment and of its nature is a venture into the relatively unknown. Culinary arts and gastronomy education has received little serious scholarly attention at graduate level to date because of the lack of theoretical underpinning that would allow it to become a discipline; because of the difficulty in separating the "industry needs" from those of "academic study" in the subject; the transitory nature and link with physical work, rather than with "science," "art," or "theory"; and because the absence of graduate programs in the field is a major deficiency in culinary arts and gastronomy education. This chapter offers a case for graduate diplomas and professional programs in culinary arts and gastronomy.

Graduate study in the field of culinary arts and gastronomy is a mode of learning least well defined and possibly least well understood, even by its practitioners. This mode of learning has been described by Gibbons (1998) as Mode 2. It is characterized by the emergence of a distributed knowledge production system. Within this system, research and teaching are no longer self-contained activities carried out in the relative isolation of traditional academic disciplines. It now involves graduate research described as "the academic equivalent of scaling an unclimbed peak." In culinary arts and gastronomy this difficulty cannot be exaggerated.

Graduate study in culinary arts and gastronomy comprises original investigation to advance the knowledge base and understand the discipline. It may involve the creation and development of ideas, designs, new insights, new products, or performativity processes. It may lead to new developments and new applications of knowledge, new and improved materials, devices, products, and processes. It may be relevant to the needs of industry, commerce, enterprise, or to public and voluntary sectors.

A graduate student in culinary arts and gastronomy will undertake graduate study leading to a master's or doctoral award in a topic related to her or his undergraduate discipline or professional work experience. The work, which involves research, must be carried out under the supervision and guidance of a suitably qualified full-time member of the academic staff, with an established research record and continuing contributions to the development of the discipline. The research supervisor, with her or his research expertise and commitment to the discipline, is a key person in determining the feasibility of the programs of research work proposed. However, this is an area that needs further research and development.

Each institute has its own protocols for undertaking graduate research for degrees and other graduate awards. Some of these are outlined in the following paragraphs to enable students to develop their own insights, reflect on their situations, and take responsibility for organizing their learning to achieve their ambitions.

STUDYING FOR GRADUATE DEGREES

Students engage in graduate study in culinary arts and gastronomy for a variety of reasons, including a romantic desire to make an exceptional contribution to their subject. As they progress through the process and engage with the grammar of having to focus on a specific topic and carry out repetitive tasks on their own, the initial romantic view is often challenged.

Once students decide to undertake a structured graduate program leading to a master's degree or a doctoral degree or undertake independent research leading to such a qualification they must be accepted by an institute and register. Once students register for the degree they progress their work by satisfactorily completing prescribed activities (assignments, projects, and seminar presentations), passing examination at the end of Part 1, and receiving approval for a dissertation to be submitted at the end of Part 2 on some particular aspect of the subject.

Graduate Program Committee

Students need assurance that the institute, faculty, and school in which they propose to pursue their graduate work has an established reputation for research and is committed to the development of graduate study and the welfare of the graduate student. Assuring curriculum quality in higher degrees for culinary arts and gastronomy is the responsibility of the institute through the director of faculty, the head of the department, and the program committee, as is normally the case for undergraduate programs. A graduate program committee, with specific terms of reference and responsibilities, appointed by the Institute's Academic Council is charged with assuring the quality of graduate courses and research.

The main functions of the graduate program committee in relation to quality assurance following close consultation with the faculty academic board, department head, and research supervisors, are to:

- set the criteria for admission;
- recommend to academic council the admission of applicants to the graduate registers, i.e., graduate diploma, master's, or doctoral registers;
- oversee the approval of graduate students' research theses;
- approve the supervision arrangements for the students' graduate research theses;
- monitor the progress of students entered on each of the graduate registers;
- regulate and approve any transfers between the registers;
- prescribe the format and layout of final theses;
- prescribe the examination processes in relation to theses, viva, and other forms of examination and assessment considered appropriate for graduate award; and
- generally make recommendations to academic council on matters pertaining to the conduct of graduate studies by structured programs (Duff et al., 2000a, p. 96).

Formal Planning and Application

The graduate curriculum committee is empowered to accept proposals for culinary arts and gastronomy research theses on structured graduate programs or by independent research within the range of academic disciplines and scholarship catered for within the school or faculty. Also, thesis proposals may draw on the various strengths of the Institute's wider research expertise and involvement, or with interdisciplinary research studies involving other educational institutions, social, professional, industrial, and/or artistic dimensions in a global context.

A number of sources for a research thesis proposal are first, the individual member of staff, who is keen to develop her or his area of research by having a number of people exploring different aspects of a problem, thereby creating around her or his work centers of expertise which will attract to the school/faculty visiting academics. These staff members usually become primary supervisors of the thesis. Second, of course, a thesis proposal may arise also from the interests of a prospective graduate student; and third, through collaboration between staff members; or fourth, with industrial cooperation. At the proposal stage, it is essential that the research thesis proposer(s)/supervisor(s) set out a plan of the thesis in terms of the background theory, focal theory, data, and contribution, seeking the resources required, along with the following:

- outline the aims of the research (What developments, controversies, breakthroughs are pushing forward thinking in the discipline? What contribution does this research make?);
- identify the resources available and those required (personnel, space, equipment, finances) to carry out the research in the time required;
- specify the responsibilities of the supervisor(s), graduate student(s), and any other personnel involved; and
- clarify the reporting arrangements to the head of the department/school, faculty authorities, other partners, industry and funding agencies.

At the level of the school, it is essential that the thesis proposal be assessed according to a number of criteria along the following lines:

- What is the quality of working life provided for the graduate student? Are the physical facilities, the equipment, and budget for the research adequate? What is the time available?
- Does the staff member involved possess the prerequisite academic qualifications, have a research track record and background to assure the quality of the supervision required at the level required, or will supplementary supervision be required?
- Can the research be formulated and directed in such a way as to offer the depth and breadth of intellectual and academic challenge appropriate to the level of graduate award proposed?

The qualifications, experience, and research track record of the supervisor are key elements in progressing the proposed research thesis. Another key element is the relationship between the researcher and the supervisor. Some students need to refer to their supervisors for constant support and reassurance, for feedback and direction, while others prefer to pursue their work independently. Good communication between the supervisor and her or his student is one of the most important elements of supervision. The very best supervisors are friendly, open, and supportive. They both inspire and persist in their constructive criticism of the work.

The head of the department attests to the fulfillment of all these criteria before a research project is approved and a graduate student permitted to go to work on it. At that stage also, the research supervisor should set out a more detailed plan for the research, based on the following practical aspects:

- facilities for schools to support research activities;
- the physical and technical objectives, targets, and achievement indicators, by time periods;
- the budget, expenditures, and financial targets, by month;
- the duties of the supervisor(s), graduate student(s), and any other personnel involved; and
- the reporting arrangements to supervisor, department head, school and faculty seminars, graduate research office, other partners, and funding agencies. (Duff et al., 2000a, p. 98)

Flexibility needs to be built into the plan to allow for changes, experiences, and the progress of the research. These need to be accounted for later, in periodic and annual reports.

GRADUATE STUDENT RECRUITMENT AND REGISTRATION

Graduate students are required to possess at least a second class honors primary degree in a relevant subject from a recognized academic institution, or an equivalent qualification to enter directly onto the master's register. Relevant work experience and demonstrated capacity to carry out the research work may also be taken into account in determining acceptability. These capacities can be supported by the new student preparing a small project with definite deadlines, so that supervisor and student can discuss the work and the student's feelings about it.

Direct entry onto the doctoral register is normally restricted to applicants who already possess a master's degree in an area related to that of their proposed research. Graduate students already on the master's register and working successfully at that level may apply for transfer to the doctoral register. They have to be recommended for upgrading to doctoral status by their supervisors. The procedure for upgrading varies from one institute to another and students need to inform themselves about the process in their institute.

In exceptional circumstances, an applicant who does not possess the required minimum entry qualifications for the master's register may apply for entry to that register on the basis of demonstrated aptitude and ability to carry out research work at the appropriate level. For instance, successful completion of the graduate diploma (research) may provide evidence of the aptitude and ability needed for master's level research work. Such applicants should contact the head of the department to discuss their research, professional, industrial, and/or other experience. On acceptance by the head of the department, the relevant supervisor will present the case for admission of such an applicant to the graduate research committee. When approval of registration has been given, the graduate student will be informed formally of her or his supervisor, the topic or field of study for which she or he has been accepted, and the minimum length of study time required before she or he is allowed to submit the thesis. Staying on the books in succeeding years is dependent on making adequate progress each year and a report to this effect will be made to the examinations board.

Preparation of Application for Registration

Graduate students are advised to visit and consult with the head of the department at the earliest possible moment before making a formal application for registration to the Institute. This contact allows for a thorough discussion on the proposed research between the prospective graduate student and the prospective supervisor(s). Also, it facilitates discussion on supervision and the availability of laboratory and other resources required. These discussions should also clarify the training and skills needs of prospective graduate students in order to effectively engage with the research work. Furthermore, such discussions will clarify for the applicant the appropriate graduate register for which application should be made.

Graduate students must normally provide the graduate research committee with an official transcript of her or his undergraduate academic results, originals of her or his degree(s) and/or any other diploma(s), and at least two references in support of the application. The referees selected should have either an academic or industrial/commercial background and have personal knowledge of the applicant and her or his academic qualifications and/or other relevant experience. Referees are requested to provide, in confidence, information and evaluations, attesting to the applicant's aptitude and fitness for graduate research in the particular discipline.

Assessment of Application

The graduate research committee assesses each application to ensure that:

- the applicant possesses or will possess the required qualifications or their equivalent, prior to registration;
- the proposed research program of work is appropriate for the graduate award for which the applicant wishes to register;

- the institution can provide the academic expertise, facilities, and resources required for the proposed research program; and
- provision has been made for adequate supervision of the proposed research program.

Arrangements for Supervision

Choosing a research supervisor is central to the successful completion of graduate research work. Supervisor(s) play a key role in devising research projects, guiding graduate students throughout their work, determining the specific direction of the research, setting appropriate academic standards to be attained by a student and assessing when she or he achieves them. It is highly desirable that more than one supervisor be appointed to provide the supervision of the graduate research student. This can be beneficial for the student, who can obtain advice from more than one person during the research, for the supervisors, who can share the burden and can together make more progress on the project than one alone, and for the institute, which is not compromised if a supervisor leaves during the project.

The appointment of the supervisor is made by the graduate curriculum committee, in consultation with the head of the department in which the research work is to be undertaken, and with the agreement of the proposed supervisor. The supervisor should normally be a full-time member of staff of that school. She or he should possess recognized expertise in the area of the proposed research work and should, normally, hold a qualification at least equivalent to the award being sought by the graduate student.

In addition, the supervisor should have prior experience of successful graduate research supervision at the level of the award being sought by the applicant. If the proposed supervisor does not have this necessary experience, she or he may be appointed as a supervisor, but will be supplemented by a suitably experienced advisory or mentoring supervisor appointed by the graduate curriculum committee, in consultation with the original supervisor and the head of the department. If a full-time staff member is not available to act as advisory supervisor, arrangements must be made with another academic institution for an experienced staff member to serve. In the conduct and management of the research, the original supervisor may provide the day-to-day supervision of the student's research work, but under the general guidance of the advisory supervisor who takes overall and ultimate academic responsibility for the work and assures its quality on behalf of the institute. This approach is a form of apprenticeship for research supervisors. It also acts to assure the quality of supervision for the graduate student and contributes to the assurance of the quality of the research work.

Where research work is interdisciplinary, involving more than one school of the institution, or is done in collaboration with an external organization, a second (or third) supervisor, nominated by the head of the second school or by the external organization, may be appointed by the graduate curriculum committee, with the approval of the department head primarily responsible and of the other (original and advisory) supervisors. The latter supervisor is expected to act in collaboration with the advisory and proposing supervisor(s).

The decision of the graduate course committee is communicated in writing to the applicant, to the supervisor(s), and to the department head concerned. If the decision is to reject the application, the grounds for rejection are included in this communication. The decision and any grounds for rejection are formally submitted to academic council for ratification.

Registration

Registration will take place as soon as possible after approval has been given and prior to the agreed commencement date of the structured graduate program. The period of registration is normally for the duration of the program. However, renewal of annual registration is approved by the graduate curriculum committee, on the basis of satisfactory completion of Phase 1 only. Evidence of such progress is provided by the graduate student fulfilling the requirements of Phase 1, and by the supervisor(s) in the form of progress reports submitted to the graduate curriculum committee during the year of registration. Permission to renew registration is communicated to each graduate student and re-registration takes place at the start of the following academic year.

Status of the Graduate Student

All graduate students included in the registers, whether full-time or part-time, are recognized as full students of the institution and as such are entitled to the same rights and privileges as all other students. Equally, they are subject to the general conduct and discipline regulations of the institution. Graduate students must comply with the regulations for graduate programs and in particular, the regulations for the graduate award for which they are registered.

INDUCTION AND INTEGRATION
OF THE NEW GRADUATE STUDENT

Graduate study and research is qualitatively and quantitatively different from most undergraduate programs. The new graduate student must be helped to make the transition from the undergraduate approach to the mode of thought and work of graduate study and research. The new graduate student needs to be introduced into the academic and social surroundings in which she or he will function for the next two or more years. She or he needs to be consciously integrated into that environment which includes the school and faculty, the overall institution, and the city and its geographic hinterland. At a minimum, the institute should arrange an institute-wide structured induction for newly registered research students. Every new student should be required to attend a series of workshops, meetings, or seminars led by a member of staff with particular interest in and responsibility for graduate research. It is important that new students have an identifiable academic to whom they may refer. These meetings should continue for at least one semester and should cover informative topics, such as:

- the research profile of the school, faculty, and the institute;
- graduate research regulations;
- accommodations (office and laboratory), including access arrangements and research equipment availability;
- education and training courses required;

- specific training program relating to the work of the project, research skills, and techniques of the discipline;
- background material about the specific project, research sources, library, and IT facilities;
- health, safety, and legal information;
- welfare arrangements;
- ethical considerations for research;
- research supervision arrangements, lines of responsibility, how to address issues and/or problems relating to supervision; and
- reporting arrangements, including seminars and written reports. (Duff et al., 2000a, p. 102)

CULINARY ARTS AND GASTRONOMY GRADUATES AND THE FUTURE

The power to confer degrees, which has resided until relatively recently with universities only, now allows institutes of technology in higher education to act as gatekeepers to the professions and to present a wide range of professional educational opportunities in society, including in culinary arts and gastronomy. The graduate degree becomes the passport to a permanent well-paid career, and with greater numbers participating in higher education, obtaining graduate qualifications is now even more essential.

Estimates vary as to the effective half-life (i.e., the time taken for half of an individual's skills and training to become obsolete) of the knowledge, skills, and capabilities acquired on a degree course, but in an era of rampant technological and societal change, the value of the knowledge, skills, and capabilities achieved on a three-, five-, or seven-year front-loaded degree will be unlikely to last a forty-year long career. In this context, traditional culinary arts and gastronomy disciplines shaped, reshaped, and occasionally obliterated by new developments are becoming less relevant and new knowledge bases are being constructed before our eyes. The pressure on culinary arts and gastronomy education to respond to these changing instrumental, economic, political, and technological circumstances will be difficult to resist, but the potential for a new graduate cadre in culinary arts and gastronomy to sustain a commitment to continuous self-improvement and professionalization through lifelong learning now exists. Consequently, there will be increasing emphasis on developing, in culinary arts and gastronomy undergraduates, the necessary research and study skills required to sustain a commitment to lifelong learning and to constant reeducation and retraining throughout their careers. Otherwise, the developers and the graduates of culinary arts and gastronomy curricula may face the charge that they have, in the words of T. S. Eliot (1976, p. 39), "had the experience, but missed the meaning."

Chapter 8

Implications of the Introduction of Doctorate Degrees in Culinary Arts and Gastronomy

The concept of a university doctorate, as the highest degree that can be awarded, has always been clear. It proclaims that the recipient is in command of a field of study or professional practice and can make a worthwhile contribution to it. She or he is worthy of being listened to as an equal by the appropriate university faculty or professional body. Doctoral degrees are indicators, not of personal or professional superiority, but benchmarks of intellectual achievement that are special and significant. Culinary Arts and Gastronomy is a comparatively new area for advanced university study and as such has yet to develop its own appropriate research methodologies. A doctoral degree certifying attainments of professional capabilities grounded in theoretical understandings is one way toward such development.

PhD OR ProfD

There is a growing debate concerning the meaning and essential requirements for a doctorate, and of the differences between the PhD, the EdD, and newer designations such as ProfD.

The PhD or Doctor of Philosophy originated in Germany. Its spread internationally began with the socialization of thousands of young American students into the scholarly rigors of German university education in the nineteenth century. This had a consequential development when these scholars returned to the United States. The first PhD in the United States was conferred in 1861 from Yale University (Gregory, 1995; Katz and Hartnett, 1976) and from that time, universities in the United States have pioneered new forms of graduate education, subsuming the German model, and setting trends often followed by other countries worldwide. In Ireland and Britain the PhD is a comparatively recent concept—an early twentieth-century import from America. It is criticized for being a more restricted achievement than the so-called higher doctorates of traditional British and Irish universities, since it envisages a limited amount of academic work (three years or so) (Phillips and Pugh, 1994). The U.S., U.K., and Irish approaches to PhD study have of course diversified. The former developed a system based on the "doctoral program" with students having to complete "courses" of study with accreditable outcomes as well as writing a thesis. Until recently the PhD in Ireland and the United Kingdom was almost entirely founded on a disciplinary approach which engaged the student in a number of years of independent research culminating in a thesis. This is usually concerned with a single, highly focused topic. This system has been criticized (Gibbons, 1998) as failing to provide adequate graduate training, and more frequently encouraging narrowness rather than encouraging depth. Interest in professional doctorates has grown over the past decade. It has become an acceptable alternative means of obtaining a doctorate for those who do not wish to pursue a career in academia.

The first professional doctorate offered in the United Kingdom was the Doctorate of Education (EdD), introduced by the University of Bristol in 1992, seventy years after the first EdD was awarded by Harvard University in response to an expressed need for more practitioners possessing a doctorate (Gregory, 1995; Anderson, 1983; Nelson and Coorough, 1994). Since then, the number of doctorates have grown considerably and expanded in the range of disciplines. Hoddell (2000) identified the development of professional doctorates in the following areas: Education, Clinical Psychology, Business Administration, and Engineering. Also, he pointed out that within these subject areas there are specialist options available. Maxwell and Shanahan (2000) explore the development of professional doctorates in Australia and New Zealand and examine how these have contributed to vertical diversity in the university sector in these countries.

A number of universities, for example, Durham, Newcastle, and Sheffield, among others, followed the Bristol initiative in launching their own EdD programs in 1994 and 1995. Although these developments have possibly been influenced by the more flexible training-oriented approach of the U.S. doctoral program, they reflect a more general concern to design doctoral qualifications which can be more supportive of the individual learner.

ADDRESSING THE INTRODUCTION OF ProfD DEGREES IN CULINARY ARTS AND GASTRONOMY

The introduction of the structured programs for the Doctorate in Education (EdD) was a significant development in a number of ways and offers a potential model for a ProfD Culinary Arts and Gastronomy or DCAG. These structured programs are being discussed here at a time of serious concern and reconsideration about the nature and meaning of doctoral research and study and their implications for culinary education and the type of problems that students face, particularly in the areas of definition, research, and study.

Each of the EdD programs at Bristol and Sheffield, among others, is based around a modular structure with a master's degree as a minimum entry requirement. At the University of Sheffield, 360 credits are required before the awarding of the EdD degree, 180 of which must be obtained through the completion in Part II of the program of a thesis of approximately 50,000 words which will be examined orally. To successfully complete Part I of the EdD program, a candidate must attend and complete a taught program of study typically equivalent to one year full-time or two years' part-time work: submit six pieces of coursework, each approximately 6,000 words, which should be publishable; and after examination of this coursework possess 180 credits.

Part I of the program is comprised of a research strand and an electives strand. The latter includes Education Policy, Management, and postcompulsory education as generic areas from which students can develop their own research according to their interests, for example, managing effective learning institutions; ethics; power and morality in subject groups; imperatives of change; leadership and facilitation of change; schools, people, and the community; concepts of professionalism and professionalization, among a host of others. The research strand examines a multiplicity of research methodologies both quantitative and qualitative including action-research, reflexive, ethnographic, and case study research. Part I of the program is examined at doctoral level and contributes to overall qualification. Completion of Part I is necessary before a candidate is allowed to proceed to Part II.

From discussion with some colleagues in the EdD program at Sheffield as to what the EdD means to them in their personal and professional lives, the notion that the EdD is about self-development, developing capabilities as reflective, knowledgeable practitioners, and being recognized as "an authority" in the field emerges. In some cases the EdD is seen as a license to teach at a university or to join a community of professional scholarly researchers. However, this does not mean nowadays that becoming a lecturer is the only reason for taking a doctorate, since the degree has much wider career connotations outside academia and many EdDs and PhDs do not have academic teaching posts. The concept stems from the need for a faculty member to be an authority, in full command of the subject right up to the boundaries of current knowledge, and able to extend them. The EdD program was perceived as equal in rigor but different in substance from the PhD. In actual practice, the distinction in program and type of dissertation is not always clear.

In the context of the increased move toward taught professional doctorates and some reactionary forces within the higher education establishment a number of questions need to be addressed. These are: What differences are there between PhD and ProfD? Why would individuals choose a ProfD? How would the ProfD benefit culinary arts and gastronomy?

Culinary arts have developed through a technical or vocational education in the field (see Airey and Tribe, 2000). Although this has been an important means of encouraging "education for culinary work," that is, orienting the organization and curricula of culinary schools toward vocational and industry needs, it has proven to be insufficient in the development of the subject or meeting the requirements for the professionalization of the practice. The belief that education should attempt to meet the needs of employers and employment is not a new one (Wellington, 1993). This vocational imperative has been around for a very long time. However, there has often been some tension in such policy initiatives between addressing the alleged requirements for "work" and meeting the accepted criteria for "education." This tension may be expressed in terms both of control and language, as groups representing educational and industry interests compete for involvement and influence while expressing themselves in words with different meanings. It is also likely to precipitate debate over the kind of curriculum appropriate for both types of concern. Such tensions and problems have led to contrasting beliefs and differing philosophies about the purpose of education.

Much criticism has been voiced over the failure of professional cookery programs to prepare students more actively for the "real world of restaurant work." Education and training for work in the industry has been associated with the preparation for jobs, tasks, and skills that would improve economic and industry performance, but the academic traditions of undergraduate education are said to have neglected or downgraded such preparation. This contributes to the views expressed by many culinary and restaurant practitioners that theoretical engagement with the subject is worth little in comparison with learning on the job. Rach (1992) stated that the establishment of a doctoral curriculum that had the support of academicians would assist the professional and academic development of the field. She points out that the professionalization of other fields including agriculture, business, education, health, and public administration have been strengthened by the development of doctoral level studies.

The concept of a doctoral curriculum for culinary arts and gastronomy (ProfD Culinary Arts and Gastronomy, or DCAG) is addressed in this context of rethinking education and training in the general field, but it is recognized from the start that this is problematic. There is no single meaning for the terms "culinary" (let alone the term "curriculum"), different definitions emerge to serve different purposes, and the likelihood of an agreed definition emerging is also problematic.

DIFFERENTIATING ProfD FROM PhD

The question of differentiation of ProfD from PhD is really concerned with the purpose of doctoral study, and is informed by the perception that the PhD is a scholar's degree and the ProfD a practitioner's:

> PhD programs involve scholarly and research activity directed
> mainly toward the acquisition of new and fundamental knowl-
> edge . . . and are distinguished from practitioner oriented doc-
> torates which prepare for the application or the transmission of
> existing knowledge and that may be intended to serve as prepa-
> ration for professional practice. PhD programs lead the student
> to focus on what he or she can do to the subject: professional de-
> gree programs are more concerned with what students can do
> with the subject. (Association of Graduate Schools, 1979)

However, Brown (1985) discovered no differences in the goals of EdD
and PhD programs. Both, he determined, had important research focuses with minimal qualitative differences. Anderson (1983) argues
that not only were the degrees exhibiting congruence in their aims,
but that the association of the PhD with researchers and the EdD with
practitioners was extremely blurred. A similar situation is likely to
exist for the proposed ProfD Culinary Arts and Gastronomy.

Gregory (1995) raises two serious issues for any discipline aspir-
ing to create the opportunity for doctoral study. The first is a challenge to those who propose a ProfD. If the aim of both these and the
PhD are apparently not dissimilar, why not simply offer a professional PhD alongside a traditional PhD without any special regulations, especially when the PhD has international recognition and currency? The second issue is whether an EdD or ProfD has less value
than a PhD because these are not there for intellectuals but for the
practical professional worker? Both of these issues strike at the heart
of the debate about the nature of doctoral study.

THE NATURE OF PROFESSIONAL
DOCTORAL STUDY IN CULINARY ARTS

The traditional view of doctoral study is one of apprenticeship "to
do research." This notion is predicated on the assumption that the
doctorate is a guarantee that its possessor will be successful as a
teacher. Doubts have been cast on the capability of PhD training to
produce effective teachers of undergraduates (Phillips and Pugh,
1994; Hartnett and Katz, 1977). Also, there were doubts about the
value of doctoral training to academic life and that such studies had a

narrowing effect on individual students. An alternative perspective is that doctoral study leads to authorship.

The introduction of EdDs and other ProfDs demonstrates the emancipation and empowerment of a growing number of senior managers and professionals in a variety of fields who seek to validate their own capabilities, expertise, and experience in the arena of intellectual endeavor. Often these doctoral candidates bring to the study their own practice and leadership skills. These are often greater in specific areas than those of the university tutor who will supervise their research.

These issues have serious implications for the introduction of ProfD Culinary Arts and Gastronomy. For example, the professional doctoral student is likely to challenge the whole university doctoral structure, support, and process. The proposed ProfD Culinary Arts and Gastronomy itself offers an interesting medium for research on the effects of such a program, and why students would wish to choose a ProfD rather than a PhD. Also, will a new model for the proposed ProfD Culinary Arts and Gastronomy emerge which would contain a redefinition of scholarly endeavor—should doctoral study in culinary arts and gastronomy be in equal measure about developing "professional scholars" as well as "scholarly professionals?" Furthermore, how should the doctoral experience be transformative of the individual, and to what extent is such study capable of achieving such transformation?

Many universities offering professional degrees also provide supervision for PhD students. The niche for the professional doctorate is expressed in its aims. These are clearly spelled out in the prospectus for the DBA at the University of Hull, United Kingdom:

> The DBA program offered by the University offers an opportunity to managers who wish to extend themselves intellectually and prepare themselves, and their organizations for the challenges of the contemporary business environment. The program builds upon course members' previous postgraduate studies and demands intellectual ability coupled with determination and creativity. (University of Hull, 1998)

The aims of the DBA program are to develop intellectual and managerial skills beyond the master's level in ways which enhance knowledge and research ability and to contribute to the advancement of knowledge and the individual's effectiveness to manage (University of Hull, 1998). This is a clear and distinctive message. It is a marketing message proclaiming the relevance of the degree to the consumer at whom it is pitched, namely, to managers who wish to extend themselves intellectually, and prepare themselves and their organizations for the challenges of the contemporary business environment. This prospect has a worrying aspect in that this program seems to suffer from short-termism and instrumentalism which should not be the sole influence for a ProfD Culinary Arts and Gastronomy. Therefore, to minimize these effects, the ProfD Culinary Arts and Gastronomy should entail not merely a change of pattern but more importantly a change of philosophy, that is, a paradigm shift from the "primacy of instrumental reason" to humanism, and from one-sidedness to all-encompassing policies (Wang, 2000, p. 223). In such an environment, culinary professionals will challenge the control of the curriculum which up to now has been largely exercised by others, e.g., bureaucrats, sociologists, and business managers who frequently specialize in culinary arts and hospitality or whose experience in the delivery and management of food service processes or products is limited or lacks currency. The ProfD Culinary Arts and Gastronomy is proposed for the practitioner seeking to achieve the highest academic credential for her or his work and professional interest, and its purpose is the same as any other doctorate: to train intellectual leaders who are highly skilled in reflexive critical inquiry and dedicated to its importance.

PROCESS AND PRODUCT IN DOCTORAL STUDY

People engage in doctoral study for reasons of preparation or continuation of their careers, for personal reasons, to become better professional practitioners, or to become professional researchers. One of the most common aims at the beginning is the wish to make a significant contribution to the chosen field. In these cases, students have become particularly interested in a topic during the course of their undergraduate degrees or while working in their profession and wish to add something to the current state of knowledge or to engage with a particular issue. The notion that any one form of doctoral achievement is superior to another fails to appreciate the transformative purposes of any such study at this highest of levels, and of the generic professional aspects of academic leadership and research, such as the focus on reflexivity, critical thinking, originality, high levels of communication of new ideas, and the ability to stimulate others toward innovation.

The proposed ProfD Culinary Arts and Gastronomy would provide excellent opportunities—if grasped—for developing linkage between the culinary industry and academia and opportunities for creating significant research. It must also be borne in mind that the ProfD Culinary Arts and Gastronomy candidates are likely to be "worldly wise" and "experienced." They will bring to the endeavor very different research issues than would the younger, less experienced PhD student. ProfD research is concerned with the immediate needs of people in particular situations of professional practice. It is important that these programs are not focused solely on the "here and now" aspects of culinary practice nor with the technical competences of research skills but with developing in ProfD students the capability to draw together concepts, relations, and principles so that fundamental understandings and synthesis can be achieved, leading to advancement in practice through the application of knowledge which is intellectual, critical, and creative.

The proposed ProfD Culinary Arts and Gastronomy offers an excellent opportunity to investigate how creative research in culinary arts and gastronomy can be encouraged, supported, and defended in the current climate. It is also to be welcomed as an innovation which offers significant degree and potential to bridge what universities have been able to offer in continuing professional development (CPD) and lifelong learning for senior and experienced practitioners and what future culinary arts and gastronomy development actually requires.

Bibliography

Adams, A. and Crawford, N. (1992). *Bullying at Work*. London: Virago Press.

Admissions Office (AO) (1998). Correspondence advising that the BA in culinary arts will not commence in 1998. Dublin: Dublin Institute of Technology.

Admissions Office (AO) (1999). Correspondence advising that the BA in culinary arts will commence in 1999. Dublin: Dublin Institute of Technology.

Aides minutes of school meetings (1996-2000). Dublin Institute of Technology.

Airey, D. and Tribe, J. (2000). Education for hospitality. In Lashley, C. and Morrison, A. (Eds.), *In Search of Hospitality: Theoretical Perspectives and Debate* (pp. 276-292). Oxford: Butterworth Heinemann.

Alvesson, M. and Skoldberg, K. (2000). *Reflexive Methodology: New Vistas for Qualitative Research*. London: Sage.

Anderson, D. (1983). Differentation of EdD and PhD in education. *Journal of Teacher Education,* 34: 55-58.

Anderson, N. (1964). *Dimensions of Work: The Sociology of a Work Culture*. New York: McKay.

Anonymous (1994). Lifestyle survey part 1: The painful truth. *Caterer and Hotelkeeper,* 30(6): 60-62.

Anonymous (1995). Violence must be controlled. *Caterer and Hotelkeeper,* 5(10): 25.

Anonymous (1998). If you can't stand the heat! . . . Kitchen violence and culinary art. *International Journal of Hospitality Management*. London: Pergamon Press.

Aristotle (1985). *Nicomachean Ethics*. Translated by Irwin, T. Indiana: Hackett Publishing Company.

Ashmore, M. (1985). A question of reflexivity: Wrighting sociology of scientific knowledge. DPhil Thesis, University of York.

Association of Graduate Schools (1979). *The Degree of Doctor of Philosophy: A Statement of Policy*. Washington, DC: Association of Graduate Schools.

Baldridge, J.V. (1983). Rules for Machiavellian change agent: Transforming the entrenched professional organisation. In *Dynamics of Organisational Change in Education* (pp. 209-219). California: McCutchan.

Ball, S. (1999). Industrial training or new vocationalism? Structures and discourses. In Flude, M. and Sieminski, S. (Eds.), *Education, Training and the Future of Work II: Developments in Vocational Education and Training* (pp. 57-77). London: Routledge in association with the Open University Press.

Barrow, R. (1984). *Giving Teaching Back to Teachers*. New York: Harvester and Wheatsheaf.

Bassey, M. (1995). *Creating Education Through Research: A Global Perspective of Educational Research for the 21st Century.* Edinburgh/Newark: British Educational Research Association/Kirklington Moor Press.

Bassey, M. (1999). *Case Study Research in Educational Settings.* Buckingham: Open University Press.

Bates, I. (1989). Versions of vocationalism: An analysis of social and political influences on curriculum policy and practices. *British Journal of Sociology of Education,* 10(2): 215-231.

Bates, I. (1999). The competence and outcomes movement: The landscape of research. In Flude, M. and Sieminski, S. (Eds.), *Education, Training and the Future of Work II: Developments in Vocational Education and Training* (pp. 98-123). London: Routledge in association with the Open University Press.

Bates, I. and Dunston, J. (1995). A Bermuda triangle? A case study of competence-based vocational training. *British Journal of Education and Work,* 18(2): 41-59.

Bell, J. (1993). *Doing Your Research Project: A Guide for First-Time Researchers in Education and Social Science.* Buckingham: Open University Press.

Blase, J. (Ed.) (1991). *The Politics of Life in Schools: Power, Conflict, and Cooperation.* Newbury Park, CA: Sage.

Blase, J. (1998). The micropolitics of educational change. In Hargreaves, A. (Ed.), *International Handbook of Educational Change* (pp. 544-557). London: Kluwer Academic Publishers.

Bloom, B., Krathwol, D., and Masia, B. (1956). *Taxonomy of Educational Objectives, 1: Cognitive Domain.* New York: Longmans.

Bobbitt, F. (1918). *The Curriculum.* Boston: Houghton Mifflin.

Boud, D., Keogh, R., and Walker, D. (1985). What is reflection in learning? In Boud, D., Keogh, R., and Walker, D. (Eds.), *Reflection: Turning Experience into Learning.* London: Kogan Page.

Bourdain, A. (2001). *Kitchen Confidential: Adventures in the Culinary Underbelly.* London: Bloomsbury Publishing.

Bourdieu, P. and Wacquant, L.J.D. (1992). *An Invitation to Reflexive Sociology.* Cambridge: Polity Press.

Boyd, W. (1921). *The History of Western Education.* London: A and C Black.

Brannen, J. (Ed.) (1992). *Mixing Methods: Qualitative and Quantitative Research.* Aldershot: Gower.

Breathnach, N. (1997). *Debate in Seanad Eireann on Draft Order Conferring Degree-Awarding Status on the Dublin Institute of Technology.* Dublin: Government Publications Office.

Brennan, J. and Shah, T. (2000). *Managing Quality in Higher Education: An International Perspective on Institutional Assessment and Change.* Buckingham: OECD, SRHE, and Open University Press.

Britzman, D. (1985). Reality and ritual: An ethnographic study of student teachers. Unpublished PhD thesis, School of Education, University of Massachusetts.

Brookfield, S.D. (1995). *Becoming a Critically Reflective Teacher.* San Francisco: Jossey-Bass.

Brown, G.A. and Atkins, M.J. (1988). *Effective Teaching in Higher Education.* London: Metheun.

Brown, L. (1985). The structure and content of doctoral study in education from the perspective of students, alumni, faculty and deans. In Brown, L. (Ed.), *The Quality of the Doctorate in Schools of Education: A Final Report to the Ford Foundation.* Ford Foundation Library.

Brownlow, J. and Dawson, J. (1995). "The Big Story: Take Three Violent Chefs." Twenty Twenty Television 28/10.

Bryman, A. (1995). *Disney and His Worlds.* London: Routledge.

Bucher, R. and Strauss, A. (1961). Professions in Process. *American Journal of Sociology,* 66: 325-346.

Bull, H. (1985). The use of behavioural objectives—A moral issue? In *Journal of Further and Higher Education,* 9(1): 74-80.

Burgess, R. (Ed.) (1984). *The Research Process in Educational Settings: Ten Case Studies.* London: The Falmer Press.

Burgess, R. (1985). In the company of teachers: Key informants and the study of a comprehensive school. In Burgess, R. (Ed.), *Strategies of Educational Research* (pp. 142-165). Lewes: The Falmer Press.

Burgess, R. (Ed.) (1989). *The Ethics of Educational Research.* London: The Falmer Press.

Carr, W. (1993). Education and the world of work: Clarifying the contemporary debate. In Wellington, J. (Ed.), *The Work Related Curriculum Challenging the Vocational Imperative* (pp. 221-223). London: Kogan Page.

Carr, W. (1995). *For Education: Towards Critical Educational Inquiry.* Buckingham: Open University Press.

Carr, W. and Kemmis, S. (1986). *Becoming Critical: Education, Knowledge and Action Research.* Lewes: The Falmer Press.

CERT (1998). Annual Report. Dublin: Council for Education, Recruitment, and Training for Hotel Industry.

CERT (2000). *CERT Statement of Strategy 2000-2006.* Dublin: CERT.

Chalk, R., Frankel, M.S., and Chafer, B.S. (1980). *AAAS Professional Ethics Activities in the Scientific and Engineering Societies.* Washington, DC: American Association for the Advancement of Science.

Chivers, T.S. (1972). Chefs and Cooks. Unpublished PhD Thesis, University of London.

Chomsky, N. (1988). Towards a humanistic conception of education and work. In Corson, D.J. (Eds.), *Education for Work: Background to Policy and Curriculum.* Palmerston North, NZ: Dunmore Press.

City of Dublin Vocational Education Committee (CDVEC) (1936). *Organisation and Development of the Scheme of Technical Education, Interim Report of the Board of Studies Committee.* Dublin: City of Dublin Vocational Education Committee.

Clancy, P. (1988). *Who Goes to College?* Dublin: Higher Education Authority.

Clancy, P. (1995). *Access to College: Patterns of Continuity and Change.* Dublin: Higher Education Authority.

Clegg, S. and Hardy, C. (1996). Some dare to call it power. In Clegg, S., Hardy, C., and Nord, W. (Eds.), *Handbook of Organisational Studies.* London: Sage.

Collins, R. (1979). *The Credential Society.* New York: Academic Press.

Corson, D. (1988a). *Education for Work.* Palmerston North, New Zealand: The Dunmore Press.

Corson, D. (1988b). Introduction: The meaning and place of work. In Corson, D.J. (Ed.), *Education for Work: Background to Policy and Curriculum* (pp. 11-18). Palmerston North, New Zealand: Dunmore Press.

Cox, R. (1980). Social forces, states and world orders. *Millennium: Journal of International Studies,* 10(2): 126-155.

Cullen, N. (1999). Personal communication, March 22.

Cuningham, G. and Walshe, J. (1998). Culinary students left out in cold by canceled course. *Irish Independent,* August 26.

Department of Education (1989). *Report of the Committee established to examine third-level courses which lead to awards by the NCEA and other bodies outside the universities.* Dublin: Government Publications Office.

Department of Education (1992). *Education for a Changing World.* Green Paper on Education. Dublin: Stationery Office.

Department of Education (1995). *Charting Our Education Future.* White Paper on Education. Dublin: Stationery Office.

Department of Education and Science (DES) (1998). Correspondence with secretary DIT re: culinary arts degree programme proposed for September 1998. August 12.

Dewey, J. (1916). *Democracy and Education.* New York: Ann Arbor.

Dewey, J. [1925] (1981). Experience and nature. Reprinted in Boydston, J.A. (Ed.), *John Dewey: The Later Works, 1925-1953,*Volume 1, Carbondale, IL: Southern Illinois University Press.

Dickinson, H. and Erben, M. (1984). Moral positioning and occupational socialisation in the training of hairdressers, secretaries and caterers. *Journal of Moral Education,* 13: 49-55.

Drummond, I., Alderson, K., Nixon, I., and Wilthshire, J. (1999). *Managing Curriculum Change in Higher Education: Realising Good Practice in Key Skills Development.* Newcastle: University of Newcastle.

Dublin Institute of Technology (DIT) (1995). *DIT Quality Assurance Handbook.* Dublin: DIT internal publication.

Dublin Institute of Technology (DIT) (1997). *DIT Quality Assurance Handbook.* Dublin: DIT internal publication.

Duff, T., Hegarty, J., and Hussey, M. (2000a). *Academic Quality Assurance in Irish Higher Education: Elements of a Handbook.* Dublin: Blackhall.

Duff, T., Hegarty, J., and Hussey, M. (2000b). *The Story of the Dublin Institute of Technology.* Dublin: Blackhall.

Durkheim, E. (1960). *The Division of Labour in Society.* New York: Free Press of Glencoe.

Eggleston, J. (1977). *The Sociology of the School Curriculum.* London: Routledge.

Eliot, T. S. (1976). *Four Quartets: The Dry Salvages.* London: Faber and Faber.

Engestrom, Y. (1993). Development studies of work as a testbench of activity theory: The case of primary care medical practice. In Chaiklin, S. and Lave, J. (Eds.), *Understanding Practice Perspectives on Activity and Context.* Cambridge: Cambridge University Press.

Eraut, M. (1989). Initial teacher training and the NCVQ model. In Burke, J.W. (Ed.), *Competency Based Education and Training* (p. 184). Lewes: The Falmer Press.

Eraut, M. (1994). *Developing Professional Knowledge and Competence.* London: The Falmer Press.

Erraught, E. (1998). Recognition of the Gap in the Training and Education Provision for Head Chefs. Unpublished MS Education and Training Thesis, Dublin City University.

Escoffier, G.A. (1903). *A Guide to Modern Cookery.* London: Hutchinson.

European Commission (1995). *White Paper: Teaching and Learning: Towards a Learning Society.* Luxembourg: Office for Official Publications of the European Communities.

Fernandez-Armesto, F. (2001). *Food: A History.* London: Macmillan.

Field, J. (1999). Reality testing in the workplace: Are NVQs employment led? In Flude, M. and Sieminski, S. (Eds.), *Education, Training and the Future of Work II: Developments in Vocational Education and Training* (pp. 124-142). London: Routledge in association with the Open University Press.

Fine, G.A. (1987). Working cooks: The dynamics of professional kitchens. *Current Research on Occupations and Professions,* 4: 141-158.

Fine, G.A. (1996). *Kitchen: The Culture of Restaurant Work.* Berkeley: University of California Press.

Fine, M. (1994). Working with hyphens: Reinventing self and other in qualitative research. In Denzin, N.K. and Lincoln, Y.S. (Eds.), *Handbook of Qualitative Research* (pp. 70-82). London: Sage.

Finegold, D. (1999). Education training and economic performance in comparative perspective. In Flude, M. and Sieminski, S. (Eds.), *Education, Training and the Future of Work II: Developments in Vocational Education and Training* (pp. 31-43). London: Routledge in association with the Open University Press.

Flude, M. and Sieminski, S. (Eds.) (1999). *Education, Training and the Future of Work II: Developments in Vocational Education and Training.* London: Routledge in association with the Open University Press.

Gibbons, M. (1998). Higher education relevance in the 21st century. Contribution to the UNESCO World Conference on Higher Education, Paris, France, October 5-9.

Gillingham, D. (1997). Correspondence in relation to European Credit Transfer System (ECTS).

Gipps, C. (1994). *Beyond Testing: Towards a Theory of Educational Assessment.* London: The Falmer Press.

Gipps, C. (1996). *Assessment for the Millennium: Form, Function and Feedback.* London: University of London, Institute of Education.

Glaser, B.G. and Strauss, A.L. (1967). *The Discovery of Grounded Theory: Strategies for Qualitative Research.* Chicago: Aldine Publishing Company.

Gleeson, D. (1990). Skills training and its alternatives. In Gleeson, D. (Ed.), *Training and Its Alternatives* (pp. 187-199). Buckingham: Open University.

Gleeson, D. and Hodkinson, P. (1999). Ideology and curriculum policy: GNVQ and mass post-compulsory education in England and Wales. In Flude, M. and Sieminski, S. (Eds.), *Education, Training and the Future of Work II: Developments in Vocational Education and Training* (pp. 158-173): London: Routledge in association with the Open University Press.

Goffman, E. (1959). *The Presentation of the Self in Everyday Life.* Harmondsworth: Penguin.

Goodson, I. (1981). Becoming an academic subject: Patterns of explanation and evolution. *British Journal of Sociology of Education,* 2(2).

Goodson, I. (1993). *School Subjects and Curriculum Change.* New York: The Falmer Press.

Goodson, I. (1998). *Subject Knowledge: Readings for the Study of School Subjects.* New York: The Falmer Press.

Goodson, I. and Hargreaves, A. (Eds.) (1996). *Teachers' Professional Lives.* London: The Falmer Press.

Governing Body, DIT (1994). *Faculty Structures.* Internal Publication.

Grace, G. (1989). Education: Commodity or public good? *British Journal of Educational Studies,* 37(3): 207-221.

Gregory, M. (1995). Implications for the introduction of the Doctor of Education degree in British universities: Can the EdD reach parts the PhD cannot? *The Vocational Aspect of Education,* 47(2): 177-188.

Guile, M. and Young, M. (1998). Apprenticeship as a conceptual basis for a social theory of learning, *Journal of Vocational Training and Learning,* 50(2): 173.

Gunnigle, P., Heraty, N., and Morely, M. (1997). *Personnel and Human Resources Management: Theory and Practice.* Dublin: Gill and Macmillan.

Habermas, J. (1972). *Knowledge and Human Interests.* London: Butterworth Heinemann.

Habermas, J. (1984). *Theory of Communicative Action,* Volume 1, Reason and the Rationalisation of Society. Boston: Beacon Press.

Hammersley, M. (1992). *What's Wrong with Ethnography?* London: Routledge.

Hargreaves, A. (1994). *Changing Teachers, Changing Times.* London: Cassell.

Hargreaves, A. and Goodson, I. (1996). Teachers' professional lives: Aspirations and actualities. In Goodson, I. and Hargreaves, A. (Eds.), *Teachers' Professional Lives* (pp. 1-27). London: The Falmer Press.

Hargreaves, D.H. (1996). Teaching as a research-based profession: Possibilities and prospects. Teacher Training Agency Annual Lecture.

Hartnett, R. and Katz, J. (1977). The education of graduate students. *Journal of Higher Education,* 48: 646-665.

Hawkins, P. and Winter, J. (1995a). *Mastering Change—Learning the Lessons of the Enterprise in Higher Education Initiative.* Sheffield: Department for Education and Employment.

Hawkins, P. and Winter, J. (1995b). *Skills for Graduates for the 21st Century.* Cambridge: Association of Graduate Recruiters.

Hegarty, J. (1996). Diploma/degree in culinary arts and cultural studies. Unpublished internal communication.

Hegarty, J. (1997). EthnoCulinary Arts—Form and Substance. Paper delivered at CHRIE International Conference, Culinary SIG, Providence, RI.

Hegarty, J. (1999). Culinary arts comes in from the cold. *Hotel and Catering Review,* August: 11-13.

Hegarty, J. (2001). Standing the heat: A case study of culinary arts curriculum development in higher education. Unpublished EdD Thesis, The University of Sheffield.

Helsby, G. and McCulloch, G. (1996). Teacher professionalism and curriculum control. In Goodson, I. and Hargreaves, D. (Eds.), *Teachers' Professional Lives.* London: The Falmer Press.

Heraty, N., Morley, M., and McCarthy, A. (2000). Vocational education and training: Institutional reform and policy developments since the 1960s. *Journal of Vocational Education and Training,* 52: 177-198.

Herbodeau, E. and Tholamas, P. (1995). *Georges Auguste Escoffier.* London: Practical Press.

Higher Education Authority (HEA) (1995). *Report of the Steering Committee on the Future Development of Higher Education.* Dublin: HEA.

Higher Education Authority (HEA) (1999). *Recommendations of HEA to Government.* Dublin: HEA.

Higher Education Quality Council: Quality Enhancement Group (1997). What are graduates? Clarifying the attributes of "graduateness." *DeLiberations* at <http://www.lgu.ac.uk/dileberations/graduates/starter.html>, August 14, 1998.

Hirst, P. (1965). Liberal education and the nature of knowledge. In Archambault, R. (Ed.), *Philosophical Analysis and Education.* London: Routledge and Kegan Paul.

Hirst, P.H. (1974). The forms of knowledge re-visited. In Hirst, P.H. (Ed.), *Knowledge and the Curriculum.* London: Routledge and Kegan Paul.

Hirst, P. and Peters, R. (1966). *The Logic of Education.* London: Routledge and Kegan Paul.

Hoddell. S. (2000). The professional doctorate and the Phd—Converging or diverging lines. Paper delivered at the Annual Conference of SHRE, University of Leicester, December 21.

Hodder, I. (1994). The interpretation of documents and material culture. In Denzin, N.K. and Lincoln, Y.S. (Eds.), *Handbook of Qualitative Research* (pp. 393-402). London: Sage.

Hodkinson, P. and Issitt, M. (Eds.) (1995). *The Challenge of Competence: Professionalism Through Vocational Education and Training.* London: Cassell.

Hoyle, E. (1981). The Politics of School Management. In *Management and the School E323* Block 3 Milton Keynes, Open University.

Hutton, W. (2001). Sir must be his own master. *The Observer,* Sunday, April 15.

Hyland, T. (1994). Silk purses and sows' ears: NVQs, GNVQs and experiential learning. *Cambridge Journal of Education,* 24(2): 233-243.

Industrial Research and Development Advisory Committee of EU Commission (IRDAC) (1994). *Quality and Relevance the Challenge to European Education: Unlocking Europe's Human Potential.* Brussels: EU Commission.

Institute of Public Administration (IPA) (1993). Report on Consultation on DIT Faculty Structures 1992-1993. DIT Internal Publication.

International Organisation for Standardization (1994). *Quality Management and Quality Assurance Vocabulary.* Geneva: IS.

International Review Group (Nelly, D. Chair) (1998). *Report of International Review Group on DIT Application for Establishment As a University.* Dublin: HEA.

International Review Team. (McGuigan, H. Chair) (1996). *Report on Review of Quality Assurance Procedures at Dublin Institute of Technology.* Dublin: HEA.

Katz, J. and Hartnett, R. (1976). *Scholars in the Making: The Development of Graduate and Professional Students.* Cambridge: Ballinger.

Kearney, R. (1986). *Modern Movements in European Philosophy: Structuralism, Critical Theory, Phenomenology.* Manchester: Manchester University Press.

Kelly, A.V. (1989). *The Curriculum: Theory and Practice.* London: Chapman.

Kennedy, D. (1998). The feasibility study on the assessment of practical work for leaving certificate physics and leaving certificate chemistry. In Hyland, A. (Ed.), *Innovations in Assessment in Irish Education* (pp. 117-127). Multiple Intelligences, Curriculum and Assessment Project Cork, University College, Education Department.

Kincheloe, J.L. and McLaren, P.L. (1994). Rethinking critical theory and qualitative research. In Denzin, N.K. and Lincoln, Y.S. (Eds.), *Handbook of Qualitative Research* (pp. 138-157). London: Sage.

Kolb, D.A. (1984). *Experiential Learning: Experience As a Source of Learning and Development.* Englewood Cliffs: Prentice-Hall.

Kornforffer, W. (1988). Vocational skills training in transition education: Successful practice in New Zealand. In Corson, D. (Ed.), *Education for Work* (pp. 221-231). Palmerston North, New Zealand: The Dunmore Press.

Kuhn, T.S. (1970). *The Structure of Scientific Revolutions* (Second Edition). Chicago: University of Chicago Press.

LaBoskey, V.K. (1994). *Development of Reflective Practice—A Study of Pre-Service Teachers.* New York: Teacher College Press.

Lashley, C. and Morrison, A. (Eds.) (2000). *In Search of Hospitality.* Oxford: Butterworth Heinemann.

Law, B. (1984). *Uses and Abuses of Profiling.* London: Harper and Row.

Lawn, M. (1996). *Modern Times? Work, Professionalism and Citizenship in Teaching.* London: The Falmer Press.

Lawton, D. (1996). *Beyond the National Curriculum: Teacher Professionalism and Empowerment.* London: Hodder and Stoughton.

Lawton, D. (1998). The Future of the Curriculum. In Trant, A., O'Donnabháin, D., Lawton, D., and O'Connor, T. (Eds.), *The Future of the Curriculum* (p. 18). Dublin: Curriculum Development Unit.

Layton, D. (1972). Science as general education. In *Trends in Education.*

Layton, D. (1973). *Science for the People: The Origins of the School Science Curriculum in England.* London: Allen and Unwin.

Leonard, D. (1986). Teacher empowerment in a curriculum project. *Irish Educational Studies,* 7(1).

Lewis, T. (1998). Vocational education as general education. *Curriculum Enquiry,* 28(3): 283-309.

MacDonald, J. (1977). *Curriculum Theory.* Washington, DC: Association for Supervision and Curriculum Development.

Maritain, J. (1966). *Education at the Crossroads.* New Haven and London: Yale University Press.

Mars, G. and Nicod, M. (1984). *The World of Waiters.* London: Allen and Unwin.

Marshall, C. and Rossman, G.B. (1989). *Designing Qualitative Research.* Newbury Park, CA: Sage.

Marwick, A. (1977). *Introduction to History. Units 3, 4, 5, of A 101, the Arts Foundation Course of the University.* Milton Keynes, Open University Educational Enterprises.

Maxwell, T. and Shanahan, P. (2000). Conference paper on current issues in professional doctoral education in Australia and New Zealand. University of New England.

McCarthy, M. (1998). Assessment at third level: Circling the territory. In Hyland, A. (Ed.), *Innovations in Assessment in Irish Education* (pp. 139-156). Multiple Intelligences, Curriculum and Assessment Project Cork, University College, Education Department.

McCulloch, G. (1985). The association of heads of technical schools 1951-1964. In Goodson, I. (Ed.), *Social Histories of the Secondary Curriculum Subjects for Study.* London: The Falmer Press.

McCulloch, G. (1986). Policy, politics and education: The technical and vocational education initiative. *Journal of Education Policy,* 1(1): 35-52.

McCulloch, G. (1988). Technical and vocational schooling: Education or work? In Corson, D.J. (Ed.), *Education for Work: Background to Policy and Curriculum.* Palmerston North, New Zealand: The Dunmore Press.

McCulloch, G. (1989). *The Secondary Technical School.* London: The Falmer Press.

McCulloch, G. (1990). An alternative road? Problems and possibilities of the Crowther concept. In Gleeson, D. (Ed.), *Training and Its Alternatives.* Buckingham: Open University Press.

McCulloch, G. (1998). *Failing the Ordinary Child? Theory and Practice of Working Class Secondary Education.* Buckingham: Open University Press.

McCulloch, G., Helsby, G., and Knight, P. (2000). *The Politics of Professionalism: Teachers and the Curriculum.* London: Continuum.

McGee, H. (1992). *The Curious Cook: Taking the Lid off Kitchen Facts and Fallacies.* Glasgow: HarperCollins Publishers.

McKenzie, P. (1995). Education and training: Still distinguishable? *The Vocational Aspect of Education,* 47(1): 35-49.

McMahon, F. (1999). Correspondence with author in relation to BA in culinary arts.

McMahon, F. (2000). The development of continuing education in higher education. Unpublished EdD Thesis. The University of Sheffield.

Mennell, S. (1985). *All Manners of Food.* US: Ilinni Books.

Mennell, S., Murcott, A., and van Otterloo, A. (1992). *The Sociology of Food: Eating, Diet, and Culture.* London: Sage.

Mentkowski, M., Astin, A.W., Ewell, P.T., and Moran, E.T. (1991). *Catching Theory Up with Practice: Conceptual Frameworks for Assessment.* Washington, DC: American Association for Higher Education.

Mulcahy, D.G. and O'Sullivan, D. (1989). *Irish Education Policy: Process and Substance.* Dublin: Institute of Public Administration.

Mulvey, M. (1997). Correspondence with Curriculum Team. March 13.

Musgrove, F. (1968). The contribution of sociology to the study of the curriculum. In Kerr, J.F. (Ed.), *Changing the Curriculum.* London: University of London Press.

National Council for Education Awards (1989). *DIT Cathal Brugha St. Institute Review.* Dublin: NCEA.

National Economic and Social Council (1993a). *Education and Training Policies for Economic and Social Development.* Dublin: NESC.

National Economic and Social Council (1993b). *A Strategy for Competitiveness, Growth, and Employment.* Dublin: NESC.

National Tourism Certification Board (NTCB) (1998). *Guidelines to Assessment for Programmes at Advanced Certificate Level,* Part III, pp. 2-10. Dublin: CERT.

Nelson, J. and Coorough, C. (1994). Content Analysis of the PhD versus EdD Dissertation. *Journal of Experimental Education,* 62(2): 158-168.

Newcastle University Careers Service (1995). *Core Skills Employers Look for in Graduate Recruits.* Newcastle: Newcastle University Careers Service.

Newman, J.H. (1852). The idea of a university. In Abrams, M.H. (Ed.), *The Norton Anthology of English Literature,* (pp.____) Volume 2. London: Norton.

Nicholls, A. and Nicholls, H. (1978). *Developing a Curriculum.* London: Allen and Unwin.

Nixon, J. (2001). A new professionalism for higher education? In Nicholls, G. (Ed.), *Professional Development in Higher Education: New Dimensions and Directions* (73-88). London: Kogan Page.

Nixon, J., Martin, J., McKeown, P., and Ranson, S. (1997). Towards a learning profession: Changing codes of professional practice within the "new" management of education. *British Journal of Sociology of Education,* 21(1): 5-28.

Norton, R.E. (1985). *DACUM Handbook.* National Centre for Research in Vocational Education, Ohio State University.

O'Connor, N. (1991). *Dublin College of Catering 1941-1991.* Internal Publication.

O'Connor, N. (1993). An eclectic model for curriculum development within DIT. In A Suggested Methodology for Curriculum Design and Development within a Constituent College of the Southside Institute. Unpublished MEd Thesis, University College Dublin.

Organisation for Economic Co-operation and Development (OECD) (1995). *Education at a Glance.* Paris: OECD.

Organisation for Economic Co-operation and Development (OECD) (1996). *Education and Training: Learning and Working in a Society in Flux.* Paris: OECD.

Organisation for Economic Co-operation and Development (OECD) (1998). *Redefining Tertiary Education.* Paris: OECD.

Ozga, J. (2000). *Policy Research in Educational Settings: Contested Terrain.* Buckingham: Open University Press.

Page, E.B. and Kingsford, P.W. (1971). *The Master Chefs: A History of Haute Cuisine.* London: Edward Arnold.

Pawson, R. (1999). Methodology. In Taylor, S. (Ed.), *Sociology: Issues and Debates* (pp. 14-49). London: Macmillan.

Pendleton, S. and Myles, A. (1991). *Curriculum Planning in Nursing Education: Practical Applications.* London: Edward Arnold.

Peters, R. (1966). *Ethics and Education.* London: Allen and Unwin.

Phenix, P.M. (1964). *The Realms of Meaning.* New York: McGraw-Hill.

Phillips, E. and Pugh, D. (1994). *How to Get a PhD: A Handbook for Students and Their Supervisors.* Buckingham: Open University Press.

Pratt, D. (1980). *Curriculum Design and Development.* New York: Harcourt Brace Jovanovich.

Pring, R. (1995). *Closing the Gap: Liberal Education and Vocational Preparation.* London: Hodder and Stoughton.

Program Document (1998). BA in culinary arts program submitted and approved by the Validating Panel, Dublin Institute of Technology. Dublin: Internal DIT Publication.

Purcell, K. and Pitcher, J. (1996). *Great Expectations—The New Diversity of Graduate Skills and Aspirations.* Warwick Institute of Employment Research, University of Warwick.

Rach, E. (1992). A study to analyse educational competences relevant to doctoral studies in tourism. Unpublished EdD dissertation, George Washington University.

Randall, P. (1997). *Adult Bullying: Perpetrators and Victims.* London: Routledge.

Report of Industrial Policy Review Group (Culliton, J. Chairman) (1992). *Industrial Policy for the 1990s.* Dublin: Government Publications Office.

Report on Tourism Manpower and Training (Malone, P. Chairman) (1995). *Policy for 21st Century*. Dublin: Department of Tourism Internal Publication.

Rietz, Carl A. (1961). *A Guide to the Selection, Combination and Cooking of Foods*, Volume 1. Westport, CT: The AVI Publishing Company.

Riley, M. (1994). Tracing skills accumulated through experience: A method of skill auditing. *Education and Training*, 36(8): 13-17.

Sanderson, M. (1994). *The Missing Stratum: Technical School Education in England 1900-1990s*. London: Athlone.

Schon, D.A. (1983). *The Reflective Practitioner: How Professionals Think in Action*. London: Temple Smith.

Schon, D.A. (1987). *Educating the Reflective Practitioner: Toward a New Design for Teaching and Learning in the Professions*. San Francisco: Jossey-Bass.

Schon, D.A. (Ed.) (1991). *The Reflective Turn: Case Studies in and on Educational Practice*. New York: Teachers College Press.

Schwab, J. (1969). The practical: A language for curriculum. *The School Review*, 78 (Nov): 1-23.

Schwab, J. (1978). *Science, Curriculum and Liberal Education*. Chicago: University of Chicago Press.

Scott, G. (1999). *Change Matters: Making a Difference in Education and Training*. Sydney: Allen and Unwin.

Selleck, R.J.W. (1968). *The New Education 1870-1914*. London: Pitman.

Shilling, C. (1987). Work experience as a contradictory experience. *British Journal of Sociology of Education*, 8(4): 407-424.

Shipman, M.D., Bolam, D., and Jenkins, D.R. (1974). *Inside a Curriculum Project*. London: Methuen.

Silver, H. (1983). *Education As History*. London and New York: Methuen.

Silverman, D. (1997). The logic of qualitative research. In Millar, G. and Dingwall, R. (Eds.), *Context and Method in Qualitative Research*. London: Sage.

Skilbeck, M. (1975). The school and cultural development. In Golby, M. et al. (Eds.), *Curriculum Design* (pp. 27-35). London: Croom Helm in association with Open University.

Skilbeck, M. (1982a). School-based curriculum development. In Lee, V. and Zeldin, D. (Eds.), *Planning in the Curriculum* (pp. 18-34). Sevenoaks: Hodder and Stoughton in association with Open University.

Skilbeck, M. (1982b). Three educational ideologies. In Horton, T. and Raggatt (Eds.), *Challenge and Change in the Curriculum* (pp. 7-18). Sevenoaks: Hodder and Stoughton in association with Open University.

Skilbeck, M. (1984). *School-Based Curriculum Development*. London: Harper and Row.

Skilbeck, M., Connell, H., Lowe, N., and Tait, K. (1994). *The Vocational Quest: New Directions in Education and Training*. London: Routledge.

Sneddan, D. (1915). Comment. *The New Republic*, May 5, p. 3.

Sorgule, P. (1999). Culinary education: The future of the food service industry. Paper presented to the Escoffier Foundation, France.

Soucek, V. (1994). Flexible education and new standards of communicative competence. In Kenway, J. (Ed.), *Economising Education: The Post-Fordist Directions* (pp. 90-97). Geelong, Australia: Deakin University Press.

Spang, R.L. (2000). *The Invention of the Restaurant: Paris and Modern Gastronomic Culture*. London: Harvard University Press.

Steier, F. (1991). *Research and Reflexivity*. London: Sage.

Stenhouse, L. (1975). *An Introduction to Curriculum Research and Development*. London: Heinemann.

Stenhouse, L. (1979). The problem of standards in illuminative research. *Scottish Educational Review*, 11(1).

Stenhouse, L. (1985). The process model in action: The Humanities Curriculum Project. In Ruddock, J. and Hopkins, D. (Eds.), *Research: As a Basis for Teaching* (pp. 89-91). *Readings from the Work of Lawerence Stenhouse*. London: Butterworth Heinemann.

Stenhouse, L. (1989) *An Introduction to Curriculum Design and Development*. Oxford: Heinemann.

Stevenson, D. (1997). *Review of Culinary Arts (Advanced Chefs Modules) Programmes*. Dublin: NTCB.

Sunter, C. (1998). *What It Really Takes to Be World Class*. Tafelberg: Human and Rousseau.

Swingewood, A. (1999). Sociological Theory. In Taylor, S. (Ed.), *Sociology: Issues and Debates* (pp. 50-72). London: Macmillan.

Taba, H. (1962). *Curriculum Development: Theory and Practice*. New York: Harcourt Brace and World.

TEASTAS (1997a). *Irish National Certification Authority, First Report*. Dublin: Government Publications Office.

TEASTAS (1997b). *Irish National Certification Authority, Second Report*. Dublin: Government Publications Office.

Tesch, R. (1990). *Qualitative Research: Analysis Types and Software Tools*. New York: The Falmer Press.

Thomas, W. (1976). The definition of the situation. In Coser, L. and Rosenberg, B. (Eds.), *Sociological Theory* (Fourth Edition). New York: Macmillan.

Thompson, A.A. and Strickland, A.J. (1995). *Strategic Management Concepts and Cases* (Eighth Edition). Chicago: Irwin.

Toohey, S. (1999). *Designing Courses for Higher Education*. Buckingham: The Society for Research into Higher Education and Open University Press.

Trant, A., Branson, J., Frangos, C., Geaney, F., Lawton, D., Makinen, R., Moerkamp, T., O'Donnabháin, D., Vourinen, P., Vonchen, E., and Walsh, P. (1999). *Reconciling Liberal and Vocational Education*. Dublin: Curriculum Development Unit.

Tyler, R. (1949). *Basic Principles of Curriculum and Instruction*. Chicago: University of Chicago Press.

UNESCO (1996). *Learning: The Treasure Within*. Paris: UNESCO.

University of Hull (1998). Doctor of Business Administration Prospectus.

University of Sheffield (1996). Guidelines for EdD candidates.

Validation Panel (1998). *Report on Validation Event in Relation to BA in Culinary Arts*. DIT, Office of Academic Registrar.

Wagner, A. (1999). Tertiary education and lifelong learning perspectives, findings and issues from OECD work. *Higher Education Management,* 11(1): 55-67.

Walshe, J. (1998). Anger at college as culinary course shelved. *Irish Independent,* August 22.

Walshe, J. (1999). *New Partnership in Education from Consultation to Legislation in the Nineties.* Dublin: IPA.

Wang, Ning (2000). *Tourism and Modernity: A Sociological Analysis.* Oxford: Pergamon Press.

Waring, M. (1985). To make the mind strong, rather than to make it full: Elementary school science teaching in London 1870-1904. In Goodson, I. (Ed.), *Social Histories of the Secondary Curriculum: Subjects for Study.* London: The Falmer Press.

Weiss, A. (1994). *Flamme et Festin: Une Poetic de la Cuisine.* Paris: Editions Java.

Wellington, J. (1993). *The Work Related Curriculum: Challenging the Vocational Imperative.* London: Kogan Page.

Wellington, J. (1994). How far should the post-16 curriculum be determined by the needs of employers? *The Curriculum Journal,* 5(3) (Autumn): 307-321.

White, J. (1997). *Education and the End of Work: A New Philosophy of Work and Learning.* London: Cassell.

Whitehead, A. (1962). *The Aims of Education.* London: Benn.

Wilson, V. (1997). Focus groups: A useful qualitative method for educational research? *British Education Research Journal,* 23(1): 209-216.

Wirth, Arthur G. (1988). Issues in the Vocational-Liberal Studies controversy (1900-1917): John Dewey vs. the social efficiency philosophers. In Corson, D.J. (Ed.), *Education for Work: Background to Policy and Curriculum.* Palmerston North, New Zealand: The Dunmore Press.

Woodhead, Chris (2000). *Sunday Times,* August 13.

Wringe, Colin (1988). Education, schooling, and the world of work. In Corson, D. J. (Ed.), *Education for Work: Background to Policy and Curriculum* (pp. 33-46). Palmerston North, New Zealand: The Dunmore Press.

Young, M. (1993a). A curriculum for the 21st century? Towards a new basis for overcoming academic/vocational divisions. *British Journal of Educational Studies,* 41(3): 203-222.

Young, M. (1993b). Bridging the academic/vocational divide: Two nordic case studies. *European Journal of Education,* 28(1): 209-214.

Index

Academic Quality Assurance in Irish Higher Education (Duff, Hegarty, and Hussey), 37
accreditation. *See* validation and accreditation
Airey, D., 10
Alvesson, M., 83
Anderson, D., 140
annual monitoring report, 70-78
    consideration of, 74-78
        critical self-study by program committee, 75-77
        documentation required for review event, 77-78
        modifications to program before five-year review, 75
        periodic critical self-evaluation and review, 75
    examination results, 71
    program monitoring report/quality rating, 71-74
assessments, 32-35, 57-58
Astin, A. W., 34

bachelor's degree, in culinary arts. *See* degree programs
Barrow, R., 20
Bates, I., 27
Bloom, B., 21
Bobbitt, F., 21
Brown, L., 140

Carr, W., 6, 16
CERT. *See* Council for the Education Recruitment and Training

Certificate in Culinary Arts, 38, 90
continuing professional development (CPD), 143
Council for the Education Recruitment and Training (CERT), 90
Course Quality Assurance Handbook, 90
Cox, R., 86-87
CPD. *See* continuing professional development
critical theory, 86-88
culinary arts and gastronomy
    curriculum development, 19-35
        assessment and examination of learning, 32-35
        chronology of process, 89-120
        for deep learning, 30-32
        defining curriculum, 19-20
        process, 20-29
        quality assurance, 53-79
        recognizing master performer, 30
        reflexivity, 81-88
    in curriculum implementation and management, 53-57
    doctorate, 135-143
        addressing introduction of ProfD degrees, 137-139
        differentiating ProfD from PhD, 139-140
        nature of professional doctoral study, 140-142
        PhD or ProfD debate, 135-137
        process and product in doctoral study, 142-143
    education, 1-4
    framework for new degree program, 37-51

culinary arts and gastronomy,
framework for new degree
program *(continued)*
conception, 37-38
preliminary proposal, 39-40
preparation of documentation,
41-43
validation and accreditation,
43-51
future of program graduates,
133-134
lack of scholarly attention to, 1-2
learning, teaching, and assessment
in, 108-111
master's degree, 123-134
future of, 133-134
graduate student recruitment
and registration, 128-132
induction and integration of new
students, 132-133
studying for, 124-128
new curriculum for, 2-4
as profession, 5-17
criteria for distinguishing
professional occupations,
16-17
liberal/vocational debate, 5-8
professionals, professionalism,
and professionalization, 12-16
relative importance of liberal and
vocational education, 8-12
curriculum development, 19-35
assessment and examination of
learning, 32-35
chronology of process, 89-120
change of design, 96-98
composition of validation panel,
114-116
curriculum proposal, 90-91
deciding aims and learning
outcomes, 93-96
developing beliefs, values, and
goals for program, 91-93
Easter vacation 1998, 113-114
focus groups, 99-101
four pillars of learning, 104-112

curriculum development,
chronology of process,
(continued)
Interim Report, 101-104
learning, teaching, and
assessment, 108-111
professional internship, 111-112
program philosophy, aims,
outcomes, content, and
structure, 102-104
September 1997 to January 1998,
98-101
submission to faculty academic
board subcommittee, 112-113
validation event, 116-120
Work in Progress Report, 97
for deep learning, 30-32
defining curriculum, 19-20
process, 20-29
composition of curriculum
development team, 22-24
establishing aims and objectives,
25-28
organization for team dynamics,
24-25
structure of curriculum and
content selection, 28-29
quality assurance, 53-79
annual monitoring report, 70-78
assessments, 57-58
disciplinary procedures, 67-69
examinations, 58-67
program review, 78-79
role of program committee in
operating program, 54
staff recruitment, induction, and
development, 53-54
student appeals, 69-70
student feedback, 54-56
teaching staff feedback, 56-57
termination of program, 79
recognizing master performer, 30
reflexivity, 81-88
advantage of reflective
ethnography, 83-86

curriculum development, reflexivity
(*continued*)
    problem solving or critical
        theory, 86-88
    reflection, reflective thinking,
        and, 82-83

degree programs
    chronology of curriculum
        development process, 89-120
    change of design, 96-98
    composition of validation panel,
        114-116
    curriculum proposal, 90-91
    deciding aims and learning
        outcomes, 93-96
    developing beliefs, values, and
        goals for program, 91-93
    Easter vacation 1998, 113-114
    focus groups, 99-101
    four pillars of learning, 104-112
    Interim Report, 101-104
    learning, teaching, and
        assessment, 108-111
    professional internship, 111-112
    program philosophy, aims,
        outcomes, content, and
        structure, 102-104
    September 1997 to January 1998,
        98-101
    submission to faculty academic
        board subcommittee, 112-113
    validation event, 116-120
    Work in Progress Report, 97
    doctorate, 135-43
        addressing introduction of ProfD
            degrees, 137-139
        differentiating ProfD from PhD,
            139-140
        nature of professional doctoral
            study, 140-142
        PhD or ProfD debate, 135-137
        process and product in doctoral
            study, 142-143
    framework for, 37-51

degree programs, framework for
(*continued*)
        conception, 37-38
        preliminary proposal, 39-40
        preparation of documentation,
            41-43
        validation and accreditation,
            43-51
    graduate diplomas, 123
    master's, 123-134
        future of, 133-134
        graduate student recruitment and
            registration, 128-132
        induction and integration of new
            students, 132-133
        studying for, 124-128
Dewey, J., 10
Diploma in Culinary Arts, 90
doctorate degree, in culinary arts. *See*
        degree programs
Dublin Institute of Technology (DIT),
        2-3, 20-21
Duff, T., 41
Dunston, J., 27

Eggleston, J., 20
episteme, 6-7
EthnoCulinary Arts Symposium, 2
Ewell, P. T., 34
examinations, 32-35, 58-67
    conduct, 62-63
    consideration of results, 65-66
    examination boards, 64-65
    external examiners, 60-62
    internal examiners, 58-60
    marking, 63-64
    report to school, 66-67

Form Q5. *See* annual monitoring report

gastronomy. *See* culinary arts and
        gastronomy
Gibbons, M., 123

Gleeson, D., 27
Goodson, I., 15, 32
Grace, G., 8
graduate diplomas, 123
Gregory, M., 140

Habermas, J., 33
Hargreaves, A., 15, 108
Hegarty, J., 41
Higher Education Quality Council
  (HEQC), 25-26
Hirst, P., 28-29
Hodkinson, P., 27
human interests, types of, 33
Hussey, M., 41
Hyland, T., 27

Kemmis, S., 6, 16
Krathwohl, D., 21

Lawton, D., 11
Layton, D., 31-32
Leonard, D., 57
liberal education
  importance relative to vocational
    education, 8-12
  vocational education versus, 5-8

MacDonald, J., 20
Masia, B., 21
master's degree, in culinary arts. *See*
  degree programs
McGee, H., 109
Mentkowski, M., 34
Moran, E. T., 34
Musgrove, F., 28

National Vocational Qualifications
  (NVQ), 9
Norton, R. E., 24

Organization for Economic
  Cooperation and Development
  (OECD), 8

Phenix, P. M., 12
Pratt, D., 20, 24
praxis, 6-7, 20
problem solving, 86-99
professional internship, 111-112
professionalism
  defined, 12-13
  distinctions from
    professionalization, 15
  as positive concept, 14-15
professionalization
  achieving, 14-15
  characteristics of professional
    organizations, 14
  distinctions from professionalism,
    15
professionals
  influence of, 13
  motivations of, 13-14

quality assurance, 53-79
  annual monitoring report, 70-78
  assessments, 57-58
  disciplinary procedures, 67-69
  examinations, 58-67
  program review, 78-79
  role of program committee in
    operating program, 54
  staff recruitment, induction,
    and development, 53-54
  student appeals, 69-70
  student feedback, 54-56
  teaching staff feedback, 56-57
  termination of program, 79
Quality Assurance Handbook (Dublin
  Institute of Technology), 37
Quality Assurance Procedures, 20-21
quality rating, 71-74

Rach, E., 139
reflection, 82-83
reflective ethnography
    advantage of, 83-86
    development of, 83-84
    need for humility in, 85-86
reflective thinking, 82-83
reflexivity, 81-88
    advantage of reflective ethnography,
        83-86
    problem solving or critical theory,
        86-88
    reflection, reflective thinking, and,
        82-83
Rietz, Carl A., 109

School of Culinary Arts and Food
    Technology, 2-3
Scott, G., 23
Silver, H., 6
Silverman, D., 84
Skoldberg, K., 83

Soucek, V., 8-9
Stenhouse, L., 21, 29

techne, 6-7
Toohey, S., 26, 34
Tribe, J., 10
Tyler, R., 21

validation and accreditation
    accreditation of program, 49
    approved program document, 49-50
    student handbook, 50-51
    validation event, 46-48, 107, 116-120
    validation panel, 44-46, 48-49
Validation Panel of the Dublin Institute
    of Technology, 2-3
vocational education
    importance relative to liberal
        education, 8-12
    liberal education versus, 5-8

Wirth, Arthur G., 11

THE HAWORTH HOSPITALITY PRESS®
Hospitality, Travel, and Tourism
K. S. Chon, PhD, Editor-in-Chief

STANDING THE HEAT: ASSURING CURRICULUM QUALITY IN CULINARY ARTS AND GASTRONOMY by Joseph A. Hegarty. (2003). "This text provides the genesis of a well-researched, thoughtful, rigorous, and sound theoretical framework for the enlargement and expansion of higher education programs in culinary arts and gastronomy." *John M. Antun, PhD, Founding Director, National Restaurant Institute, School of Hotel, Restaurant, and Tourism Management, University of South Carolina*

SEX AND TOURISM: JOURNEYS OF ROMANCE, LOVE, AND LUST edited by Thomas G. Bauer and Bob McKercher. (2003). "Anyone interested in or concerned about the impact of tourism on society and particularly in the developing world, should read this book. It explores a subject that has long remained ignored, almost a taboo area for many governments, institutions, and organizations. It demonstrates that the stereotyping of 'sex tourism' is too simple and travel and sex have many manifestations. The book follows its theme in an innovative and original way." *Carson L. Jenkins, PhD, Professor of International Tourism, University of Strathclyde, Glasgow, Scotland*

CONVENTION TOURISM: INTERNATIONAL RESEARCH AND INDUSTRY PERSPECTIVES edited by Karin Weber and Kye-Sung Chon. (2002). "This comprehensive book is truly global in its perspective. The text points out areas of needed research—a great starting point for graduate students, university faculty, and industry professionals alike. While the focus is mainly academic, there is a lot of meat for this burgeoning industry to chew on as well." *Patti J. Shock, CPCE, Professor and Department Chair, Tourism and Convention Administration, Harrah College of Hotel Administration, University of Nevada–Las Vegas*

CULTURAL TOURISM: THE PARTNERSHIP BETWEEN TOURISM AND CULTURAL HERITAGE MANAGEMENT by Bob McKercher and Hilary du Cros. (2002). "The book brings together concepts, perspectives, and practicalities that must be understood by both cultural heritage and tourism managers, and as such is a must-read for both." *Hisashi B. Sugaya, AICP, Former Chair, International Council of Monuments and Sites, International Scientific Committee on Cultural Tourism; Former Executive Director, Pacific Asia Travel Association Foundation, San Francisco, CA*

TOURISM IN THE ANTARCTIC: OPPORTUNITIES, CONSTRAINTS, AND FUTURE PROSPECTS by Thomas G. Bauer. (2001). "Thomas Bauer presents a wealth of detailed information on the challenges and opportunities facing tourism operators in this last great tourism frontier." *David Mercer, PhD, Associate Professor, School of Geography & Environmental Science, Monash University, Melbourne, Australia*

SERVICE QUALITY MANAGEMENT IN HOSPITALITY, TOURISM, AND LEISURE edited by Jay Kandampully, Connie Mok, and Beverley Sparks. (2001). "A must-read. . . . a treasure. . . . pulls together the work of scholars across the globe, giving you access to new ideas, international research, and industry examples from around the world." *John Bowen, Professor and Director of Graduate Studies, William F. Harrah College of Hotel Administration, University of Nevada, Las Vegas*

TOURISM IN SOUTHEAST ASIA: A NEW DIRECTION edited by K. S. (Kaye) Chon. (2000). "Presents a wide array of very topical discussions on the specific challenges facing the tourism industry in Southeast Asia. A great resource for both scholars and practitioners." *Dr. Hubert B. Van Hoof, Assistant Dean/Associate Professor, School of Hotel and Restaurant Management, Northern Arizona University*

THE PRACTICE OF GRADUATE RESEARCH IN HOSPITALITY AND TOURISM edited by K. S. Chon. (1999). "An excellent reference source for students pursuing graduate degrees in hospitality and tourism." *Connie Mok, PhD, CHE, Associate Professor, Conrad N. Hilton College of Hotel and Restaurant Management, University of Houston, Texas*

THE INTERNATIONAL HOSPITALITY MANAGEMENT BUSINESS: MANAGEMENT AND OPERATIONS by Larry Yu. (1999). "The abundant real-world examples and cases provided in the text enable readers to understand the most up-to-date developments in international hospitality business." *Zheng Gu, PhD, Associate Professor, College of Hotel Administration, University of Nevada, Las Vegas*

CONSUMER BEHAVIOR IN TRAVEL AND TOURISM by Abraham Pizam and Yoel Mansfeld. (1999). "A must for anyone who wants to take advantage of new global opportunities in this growing industry." *Bonnie J. Knutson, PhD, School of Hospitality Business, Michigan State University*

LEGALIZED CASINO GAMING IN THE UNITED STATES: THE ECONOMIC AND SOCIAL IMPACT edited by Cathy H. C. Hsu. (1999). "Brings a fresh new look at one of the areas in tourism that has not yet received careful and serious consideration in the past." *Muzaffer Uysal, PhD, Professor of Tourism Research, Virginia Polytechnic Institute and State University, Blacksburg*

HOSPITALITY MANAGEMENT EDUCATION edited by Clayton W. Barrows and Robert H. Bosselman. (1999). "Takes the mystery out of how hospitality management education programs function and serves as an excellent resource for individuals interested in pursuing the field." *Joe Perdue, CCM, CHE, Director, Executive Masters Program, College of Hotel Administration, University of Nevada, Las Vegas*

MARKETING YOUR CITY, U.S.A.: A GUIDE TO DEVELOPING A STRATEGIC TOURISM MARKETING PLAN by Ronald A. Nykiel and Elizabeth Jascolt. (1998). "An excellent guide for anyone involved in the planning and marketing of cities and regions. . . . A terrific job of synthesizing an otherwise complex procedure." *James C. Maken, PhD, Associate Professor, Babcock Graduate School of Management, Wake Forest University, Winston-Salem, North Carolina*